Rainbow Around The Son

By

Marlo Gottfurcht Longstreet

Rainbow Around The Son

Copyright © 2018 by Marlo Gottfurcht Longstreet

All Rights Reserved. No part of this publication may be reproduced, distributed, or transmitted in any form or by any means, including photocopying, recording, or other electronic or mechanical methods, including information storage and retrieval systems, without the prior written permission of the publisher, except in the case of brief quotations embodied in critical reviews and certain other noncommercial uses permitted by copyright law.

Print ISBN: 978 -1- 7326521- 0-1
Ebook ISBN: 978-1-7326521-1-8

Library of Congress Control Number: 2018953997

Printed and Bound in the USA First Printing October 2018

Published by Simply Good Press
Montclair, New Jersey 07043
www.Simplygoodpress.com

Photographs from the personal collection of
Marlo Gottfurcht Longstreet

Cover Art: Barbara Sokol
Cover Design: CG Creative Studios
Author Photograph: Lauren Fash

Acknowledgements

When my tragedy hit, my wonderful friends stuck by my side. Through joy and pain, sadness and laughter, they were there. So many stood by me. So many held my hand and wiped away my tears. So many came out of the woodwork. Friends from near and far. Friends from childhood, from camp, from high school, from college, from adult life. I will forever be grateful for you. I thank you, my many friends, from the bottom of my heart.

My deepest thanks to the incredible researchers, scientists, doctors and others who contributed to the Tanner Project Foundation. A special thank you to Dr. Craig Venter, Dr. Nicholas Schork, Dr. Laura Goetz, Dr. Victoria Magnuson, Dr. Judith Weiner and Heather Kowalski for always going above and beyond, thinking outside the box and sharing our goal in helping to keep Casey healthy.

To Jamie and Oliver Wyss – For your wisdom and friendship.

To Barbara Sokol - For perfectly capturing Tanner, hip thrust and all, in your painting, *Waiting for Fed-Ex*, which I am honored to use on the cover of my book.

To Claudio Gutierrez and your amazing team at CG Creative Studios – For your continued help and creativity.

To Annie Gilbar – I always knew I needed to find someone who believed in me, as much as I believed in myself. I always knew I needed to find someone to encourage me, edit me, help me and guide me, as I shared my story. Thank you for being that person.

To Sherry – My mom and Casey and Tanner's "Mimi." Thank you for all of your continued love, help and support. I know how hard it was for you when Tanner was sick, and I am so thankful you are healthy. And to Stan – Thank you for always being by my mom's side.

To Grant and Jackson – Thank you for your warm hearts and incredible souls. Peace and love.

To Greg – If I could handpick an ex-husband, it would be you. Vows don't matter...family does. And that's what we are. Always. Thank you for being a wonderful friend and the best dad ever to Casey and Tanner.

To Michael – Who would have thought that the night we met, at "Movies in the Park," would turn into what we have today? It's been a difficult road, but I am forever grateful to have you by my side and for all the love you give to me. Looking forward to so much more.

To Elliot – My dad and Casey and Tanner's Papa – Where do I even begin? Thank you for helping me create a Foundation that is so important to Tanner's legacy. You believe in me every single day and give me so much love, help, encouragement and support. I couldn't be where I am today if it wasn't for you. Thank you for everything.

To Casey – My daughter, my world. I am so proud of the woman you are becoming and I can't wait to see what's in store for you. You are my shining star. My love. My life. May you be safe, may you be healthy, may you be happy and may all your dreams come true. I love you with all of my heart.

To Tanner – My baby boy. I miss you every single day. Every moment of every day. Thank you for all of your love, laughter and smiles. Thank you for being my son. Thank you for making your Mama proud. Thank you for being our hero.

When I was a little girl, all I wanted was to be a Mommy. No words can describe the feeling when you become one.

To my incredible two kids, Casey and Tanner, for making my dreams come true.

xo

*Greg, Marlo, Casey and Tanner
November 2011*

Prologue

My son, Tanner, died. He was eleven. Brain Cancer. What. The. Fuck.

Even now, years later, I still don't believe it. Honestly, I don't.

When I hear about a child dying, for a split second, I think, "How terrible! I can't even imagine." But then after that second, I remember that, yes, I *can* imagine. I am that person. I am that Mom. I have lost a child. Call it shock, call it a protective mechanism, call it whatever you want. For a split second, I forget, and then I remember.

Tanner was diagnosed with one of those brain cancers that, when you hear the name, you take in a little breath and think, "It's not a good one." Glioblastoma. The name itself sounds like an evil villain in a movie. But there was more. Not only did Tanner have brain cancer, we also found out he had a hereditary cancer gene, the mutant p53. He inherited it from his dad, Greg.

My son died. I still don't understand it. How can my son be dead? How can a ten-year-old get brain cancer and die eight months later? How will I face the reality that I will never again hold, kiss, hug, feel, talk to my son?

This is my life. This is my journey. So many questions that just don't have answers, yet I still search for them daily.

You know, there's a stigma attached to a person who has lost a child. You become a member of a club that no one wants to be a part of. You become "that person." And here I am.

During Tanner's illness, death and thereafter, I wrote a lot. There was so much going on. Moments of love, of happiness, of sadness, of joy, of tears, of making painful decisions that a parent never wants to make. The writing helped me, and it helped others as well. It was my journey that I chose to share. Actually, I carefully chose what I wanted to share, and my forum was Facebook.

In the beginning, my posts were mundane. I kept it simple. And, as life got more complex, my posts became more raw and personal. Facebook became my public journal. I allowed my 900 plus friends to have a front row seat to my life. And at the same time, I also kept a private journal of my thoughts and feelings, which I would never dare share…until now. My diary. My journal. Permission to read. All of it.

Rainbow Around The Son

I write it like it is. A lot is hard core. I don't sugar coat, and for that, I am proud. I may answer your deepest darkest questions. I may address your deepest, darkest fears. Death is taboo. It's a topic no one likes to deal with or discuss. So, take that hands-off taboo topic and apply it to a kid. Taboo times, well, a lot.

Mothers aren't supposed to bury their children. Kids aren't supposed to die. So, when they do and when it happens, people don't know how to handle it. It's a topic people find awkward, difficult and painful to discuss. Some friends will openly talk about Tanner, while others sweep his death under the rug and pretend it didn't happen. Yes, death is scary, but so is life.

A friend recently said to me that I was the most proactive parent she has known, and this was describing me *before* Tanner got sick. But, as proactive as you might be, sometimes it will never be enough. When you think you have dotted all your i's and crossed all your t's, there's something still out there that you might have missed. Never did I realize the importance of genetics and genomics; the importance of advocating and of not being intimidated; the importance of going with your gut feeling, your instinct.

There's so much I will share on these pages, because there are things I know today that I didn't know then. Things I wish I had known. Things that you should know.

Marlo Gottfurcht Longstreet

Remember that hereditary cancer gene Tanner had? Our almost twenty-year-old daughter, Casey, carries the same gene and has an over 90% chance of getting cancer. Yes, you read that right.

My journey didn't end with Tanner's death. It continues by making sure Casey stays healthy. It continues by keeping Tanner's memory alive. It continues by learning to live again.

Welcome to my life…there's no turning back.

Rainbow Around The Son

May 18, 2013

A little before noon.

Tanner just died.

My baby will always be in my heart...your sweet woman will always love you.

RIP my baby boy.

For Tanner's entire life, he was in my arms. By my side. Cuddling with his Mama. During the several hours before he passed away, as the family gathered at his bedside, we took our positions. Greg was on one side of him, and I gave up my permanent spot of holding him in my arms. I gave that to Casey. I don't know why or how or what made me do that. I just did. I was on his left side next to his feet. My body faced his body. I intertwined my legs with his, just as we had slept for many a night, and I held onto his webbed toe, that I loved so. I did not let go...at all.

Eight Months Earlier...

September 2012

On September 10, 2012, my ten-year-old son, Tanner, was admitted to the hospital with a brain tumor. Two days later, on September 12, he had brain surgery.

People ask me all the time, what happened? Honestly? He just didn't feel well. He had six days of flu-like symptoms, and that was it. We had taken him back and forth to the pediatrician and she, too, thought it was probably a bad virus, or possibly meningitis, since Tanner had a headache and was lethargic. Even his blood test came back normal. Honestly, as I write this, it still seems unbelievable.

They told us to wait it out. Normal blood tests mean everything is okay, right? Tanner went through the weekend still not feeling well. He was tired, nauseous, not much appetite and the headache persisted. Truly, it was like he had a bad flu.

On that Monday morning, September 10, he still wasn't himself. Greg and I decided to take him back to the doctor. You may have already guessed that I was not the kind of mom who waited it out. One day of waiting it out was enough for me. These symptoms were not going away, were not getting better, and my child was really sick. We needed to get to the bottom of it. Greg was going to take him because I was scheduled for a root canal that morning. Totally shitty timing.

Greg took Tanner to the pediatrician, and I drove myself to my dreaded dental appointment. Both offices are in Beverly Hills, about five minutes from each other. As doctors usually do, mine was running late, meaning my root canal was not going to start on time. Just as it was about to begin, Greg called.

"Dr. Weiner wants us to take Tanner to the hospital emergency room." I bolted out of the dental office and ran to my car. I don't even remember driving to the pediatrician's office, where I met Greg. I just remember Tanner's pediatrician, Dr. Weiner, saying "something isn't right." She was smart. She knew Tanner and agreed that this was not Tanner battling a flu. You know that feeling when you just know something is very, very wrong? She felt it, and so did we.

We put Tanner in my car and Greg followed me to the hospital. I remember how out of it Tanner was and so very tired. He was sprawled across the back seat of the car, as I drove. Hardly talking. Hardly moving. This was not Tanner.

Rainbow Around The Son

We checked into the emergency room and told the emergency room doctors everything about Tanner. After describing his symptoms, they told us it sounded like meningitis. I asked, "What is the treatment?" They told me that depending on which kind of meningitis it was, he would likely have to stay in the hospital for a few days, or he might be able to go home with antibiotics. They told us they had to do a spinal tap to confirm, but before that, they would do a routine CAT scan of his brain. I never asked, "Why his brain?" I thought nothing of that. I was terrified of how he would react to a spinal tap. A CAT scan of his brain was nothing.

Tanner finished his scan and we waited in the little emergency room. He was acting a little peppier, watching the television over his bed. He just wanted to go home. I saw this as a good sign. Maybe he was feeling better. Maybe it was just a bad flu.

The emergency room doctor came in and shut the door behind her. "You need to sit down," she said quietly. It was like out of a movie or television show. You know when they tell you to sit down, it's bad news. Terrible, terrible news.

Everything was in slow motion. Know what I mean? I looked at her and said, "I will not sit down. Tell me what's going on." I remember it now like it was yesterday. I heard the words... not all of them...but the important ones. Mass. Brain. Three centimeters. ICU. Operate.

WHAT THE FUCK!!!!!!!! I wanted to SCREAM. I wanted to YELL. I was in a daze, a fog of disbelief. What the fuck did she mean…a mass on his brain? I called my parents. I called my boyfriend, Michael. I called one of my best friends, Gayle. Greg left to get Casey out of school. And somehow, I realized, for the first of many, many times that our lives as we knew them would never be the same.

The next two days were a blur. A blur of meeting doctors and surgeons. A blur of Tanner taking test after test after test. A blur of coordinating Casey's schedule. A blur of it all.

I called and told only those who were close and important in my life. I didn't want to broadcast what was going on. Not just yet. Not until I knew more. But the problem is, we live in a day and age where social media is king. My mom posted about Tanner's surgery on Facebook, and then there was no hiding. The texts, emails and calls started coming in. Honestly, I wasn't ready to deal with it publicly quite yet. I was still digesting it all.

In the end, ironically, it was Facebook that became so important in this journey. Through my posts, I was able to not only update everyone, but share my thoughts and feelings, as much or as little as I wanted. In a way, it became my therapy.

So here we were on the morning of September 12. My baby was about to have brain surgery. We all needed to come together… we all needed to be together…as a family.

Rainbow Around The Son

If anything was a true test, it was this.

I am divorced. My ex-husband, Greg, and I were together for eighteen years, thirteen of those we were married. We weren't a "bad" couple. Just the opposite. We were a good one. We just grew apart instead of growing together. In the end, I think we both realized we were at different places and couldn't meet at the same place. The one thing we did agree on was remaining friends, especially for our children.

We had been divorced for three years when Tanner got sick. We were friends, not the best of friends, not the worst of friends… just friendly friends. We were the parents of two kids we loved, and we worked together as best as we could. We had separate lives, though. We did our own thing. We didn't have to dictate to each other anymore. We didn't have to decide on rules for one another. It was just about the kids.

When Tanner got sick, and throughout the months that followed, we were thrust together. We had to learn to pick up, in a way, where we left off before our marriage ended. Except this time, we were no longer married. Once again, we had to learn how to be with each other every day. It helped that we went into this crisis as 'friendly friends,' and not as enemies. We would have to work together as a team, and make life and death decisions that no parent ever wants to face. There was one thing that was certain: we would deal with this head on, together, as a family. Married or not.

On that surgery morning, Greg and I held Tanner as they gave him a sedative. We watched him fall asleep, we kissed him, then walked into the hallway and began to sob. To leave your baby in the hands of others, to not be able to hold him during his operation, was unimaginably painful. It was excruciating not to be able to go into "Mom" mode and be there. But I had no choice...we had no choice.

Our family was in the waiting room, and we made our way back to them. As we walked down the hall, a liaison nurse met us. We told her it was important to us to have updates during the surgery. We didn't know how long it would be, and I remembered, years earlier, when my grandfather had bypass surgery, a kind nurse would tell us what was happening every hour or so. I wanted the same for us today.

We knew the surgery was to begin at 9 a.m. We took over a part of the waiting room, knowing it was going to be a long day. It was just our immediate family and our close friend, Tim. Although so many people offered to sit with us, we just didn't want anyone else there.

Suddenly, and unexpectedly, Tanner's surgeon came into the waiting room. I was confused. What was his doctor doing here?

He's supposed to be in surgery with Tanner. He held a piece of paper in his hand, which he threw on the waiting room table. For a split second, I thought the initial reports were wrong, and that Tanner didn't need surgery.

It was just the opposite. In fact, it was something I never expected.

The doctor started to yell at us. He kept motioning to the paper. We were clueless as to what this important paper was. And then we were told. This "paper" was a note from his office regarding our request for updates during the surgery (the request we had made to the liaison nurse a half hour earlier). Apparently, and unbeknownst to us, hospital protocol was that, if a request like that is made, it goes to the doctor's office, and they write a note, and it is brought to the doctor. And whoever wrote the note, miscommunicated the situation, and said we were complaining that we were not being updated on the surgery as it progressed (which, of course, made no sense since the surgery had not yet started).

The problem was that they handed the doctor the note as he was scrubbing into Tanner's surgery. We had no idea this was going to happen. The doctor was furious. Here he was ready to start surgery, and had been interrupted. I get it - he was in "game mode," and this was a distraction. But to yell at us the way he did? That was not okay. The last thing we wanted was an irate doctor operating on our son.

The nurse apologized and took the blame. We apologized as well. We just wanted the doctor to take care of Tanner. He left and the surgery started. We truly hoped this was not the start of how things were to come.

We waited. And waited. And waited. I don't remember much of those hours. Looking back, the only thing I truly remembered was thinking how we may have to install an elevator at home in case Tanner couldn't climb the stairs anymore. You know…those side elevators that go along a staircase? OMG…Tanner would have loved that. But of course, the only reason we would have had to put in an elevator would be, if Tanner couldn't walk. I didn't even want to go there.

When it was confirmed that Tanner needed brain surgery, we requested for Dr. B to be in the operating room. Dr. B is a world-renowned brain surgeon who, thankfully, worked at the hospital where Tanner was having his surgery. It was not so simple to have Dr. B as part of Tanner's surgical team: he was not a pediatric surgeon, nor did he take insurance. Thankfully, he granted our request, and he was the other set of eyes in the surgery room, along with Tanner's primary surgeon.

Rainbow Around The Son

The surgery lasted about four hours. When it was over, Tanner's surgeon (the one who was not so happy with us earlier) took us aside and told us that the surgery was a success. We were told that during the surgery two frozen samples were taken. Both samples looked benign. We were told that they had removed 100% of the tumor. But we were also told there was a lot of edema...a lot of swelling. All I could focus on, though, were those frozen, benign-looking samples. We would just have to wait for final pathology results, which we were told would take four to eight days.

We spent ten days in the hospital. I was with Tanner almost the entire time. Greg and Michael were there, too. I didn't want to leave Tanner for a moment, but I also needed to spend time with Casey. It wasn't fair to her. So, to give me a break, Greg and Michael would occasionally take care of Tanner...together (teamwork at its finest when it's your ex-husband and boyfriend). Since my mom lived so close to the hospital, she also helped with Casey. As I said, we were going to conquer this as a family.

I will always remember a moment Michael and I had during this time. We were in the hallway of the ICU, a sort of bridge that connected the ICU to the main hospital. We were looking down at the people, the cars and the traffic below. I turned to him and said, "Look at all of those people down there. For them it's just a normal day." I couldn't believe how everyone could go about their day as our life was taking a turn, not knowing what was in front of us.

After the surgery, we were told there could be a chance of paralysis. There was none. Two days after surgery, Tanner wanted to go home. He was determined to get out of the hospital. And he had a huge appetite. Hospital food? Not for this kid. I got Tanner's favorite prime rib dinner from Lawry's and snuck it into the ICU. Such a simple yet important thing to do for my child.

Tanner spent nine of those days in the ICU, and the last in a regular room. He wanted out of that hospital as soon as possible. He just wanted to go home. He kept saying, "No kids allowed" when he was in the ICU unit. Such a telling thing to say…No Kids Allowed. He was so right.

In all honesty, I truly thought this brain tumor thing was a fluke. He made it through surgery. There was no paralysis. They removed the entire tumor. And those frozen samples were thought to be benign. He was just as happy and stubborn and funny as always. He was still Tanner. I was certain that this would be a blip in his life, and that we would just have to check in with a neurologist every six months for follow-up.

Never did I think this could be the "C" word.

Rainbow Around The Son

Remember those four to eight days we were told we had to wait for pathology results? Forty-eight hours after surgery, the doctors called us into a small room. They shut the door. Memories flooded back to just a few days earlier when the emergency room doctor told us about the mass on his brain. I knew this wasn't going to be good. Good news was told in the room, with Tanner by our side. Not in a small room with the door shut.

The surgeon and a pediatric oncologist told us the news. The pathology report came back. It was a glioblastoma (GBM). I remember saying, "What happened to four to eight days? It's only been forty-eight hours. How can you be so sure?"

They said they were sure.

A glioblastoma. Whatever that was, it sounded terrible. And it was. As they explained, I was once again in a blur. I took notes not really knowing what I was writing. Cancer. Grade IV. Terminal. I was listening. But I didn't really hear. I was present. But my mind was in a million places. I was numb. My baby was sick.

We wanted more opinions. A lot more. All *they* wanted was for us to start radiation right away. We needed time to digest this. We needed time to look at every option. We needed to go home.

The day we left the hospital, they told us pathology changed their findings. It was now an anaplastic astroblastoma. A tumor, the pediatric oncologist said, she had never seen before.

In the end, it turned out that Tanner had both kinds of tumors...glioblastoma and anaplastic astroblastoma. So typical of Tanner...nothing was ever simple.

At some point, I received the operation report. Have you ever read one of those? Wow. It's literally a play-by-play of what happens during a surgery. After reading the report, we were speechless. And thankful that we had asked for Dr. B to be in the room, observing the surgery. The report gave us all of the details:

'There was a small portion of tumor that was still left superficially, posterior portion. At this point, Dr. B scrubbed into the room and began examination of the field. He resected a small approximately 4mm residual in the posterior superficial portion of the resection cavity. He then began to explore the deep portion of the resection cavity and as he was gently manipulating this area, there was a drop of the SSEP's. He immediately stopped any manipulation in this area. At this point, he confirmed that there was indeed a gross total resection. He scrubbed out of the case at this point.'

It was Dr. B that went in and finished the job. It was Dr. B that got out 100% of the tumor. (And looking back, it was most likely, because of Dr. B, that Tanner lived a good eight months post-surgery.)

The first days back at home were so normal. So normal it was scary. Tanner seemed to be okay, just fine. The only indication that he had had surgery was a large scar on the side of his head. He still had his thick head of hair.

We took the first week to just digest it all. We made appointments with other doctors. We sent the pathology to other labs. I think a part of me thought "out of sight, out of mind." I also think a part of me thought, "well, they got the whole tumor, we will do treatment, but he's going to be fine." I know now that I never understood the severity of it then. I mean, I probably did in the back of my mind. But who wants to think about their child having terminal brain cancer?

We started our journey by seeing another doctor, a pediatric neuro-oncologist, Dr. Jonathan Finlay, at Children's Hospital Los Angeles (CHLA). Looking back, never did I realize how important that visit would be and how our entire lives would change once again.

The first thing he said to us was something no one had yet asked (but should have):

"What is your family history?"

A question that is so important to this story. WHAT IS YOUR FAMILY HISTORY? It was after learning that Greg's mom had breast cancer in her early thirties (and passed away at forty-nine), that a red flag was raised. The doctor told us about the mutant p53 gene, a hereditary cancer gene that can lead to many types of cancers, including brain, breast, bone, blood, soft tissue sarcoma, adrenal cortical, melanoma, colon and more. It's called Li-Fraumeni Syndrome. It was rare, but Tanner should be tested for it.

I took notes on a yellow legal tablet. In the middle of the paper I wrote p53 and circled it. I had no idea that this p53 would change our lives forever.

Can I just say...as I think about this meeting, and Dr. Finlay asking us about our family history, I cannot believe our original hospital, the one where Tanner had his surgery, never asked us this. They never once questioned *why* a ten-year-old kid had brain cancer. They just wanted to treat it. I get it...what do you do when you fall down and hurt yourself? You bandage your wound. You don't ask why or how it happened, what you could have done differently? You just bandage, and then later, you ask the why's. Same thing here. There was an immediacy to treat Tanner's tumor, and that I understand. But you still need to ask the question.

It was important to look at the big picture. At that time, we didn't know if Tanner had the mutant gene. We were going to test for it. But if he did have it, if you have a mutant cancer gene, the treatment may not be the same than if you didn't have a mutant gene. Yes, treat the wound, but it was important to take a moment and ask: why?

Those few weeks passed and we talked to everyone. We knew what we were up against, and it wasn't good. We decided to start treatment at a local hospital with Dr. T, a pediatric neuro-oncologist. Dr. Finlay would also be on our team, consulting with Dr. T. We felt like we were in good hands with doctors who understood us.

I knew we had a long road in front of us. Thankfully, for many years, I had always worked from home. Now, more than ever, I would be able to juggle my work schedule with Tanner's needs.

We decided on a treatment plan. First, three rounds of chemotherapy. A stem cell transplant would follow and then radiation would come much later, if at all. At this time, we also tested Tanner's blood for the mutant cancer gene, p53, which Dr. Finlay had told us about.

We had hopes for Tanner. If anyone could beat this, it was him. I truly felt that way. I know so many say it, but I felt it. Tanner was a unique kid, and I swore that my son would be the one to beat this cancer.

Tanner started chemotherapy. The first round included a hospital stay. He needed to get a port surgically inserted into his chest; they also did a spinal tap to make sure the cancer had not spread into his spine. The port was inserted successfully, and there was no spread of cancer. Finally, some good news. First round went without a hitch…with the exception of a call we received.

Right before Tanner was to start chemotherapy, we got a call from Tanner's primary surgeon (from the original hospital where his surgery had taken place). He told us we were making a mistake and disagreed with our course of treatment. He was adamant that we should start radiation, not chemotherapy. He basically made us question our treatment decision for Tanner. We were already two scared parents making important decisions for our son. For him to call us, as he did, was simply horrible. Seriously, what the fuck?

When Greg and I decided on a treatment plan, we had met with a radiation oncologist at the hospital. I asked him the typical question: If this was your kid, what would *you* do? He said no radiation, at least not right away. Chemotherapy and stem cell therapy were our first course of action. Radiation would come much later. If we were to do radiation, it would be after chemotherapy, when the area to be radiated was much smaller. Radiating such a big part of Tanner's brain would most likely cause harm to his brain function. Radiation, at this time, was absolutely not an option.

We went ahead according to our plan. We were Tanner's parents and felt we were making the right decision, the right course of action for Tanner. Tanner's oncologists, Dr. T and Dr. Finlay, were also in agreement. We would not let the opinion of his surgeon sway us differently. And so, treatment began.

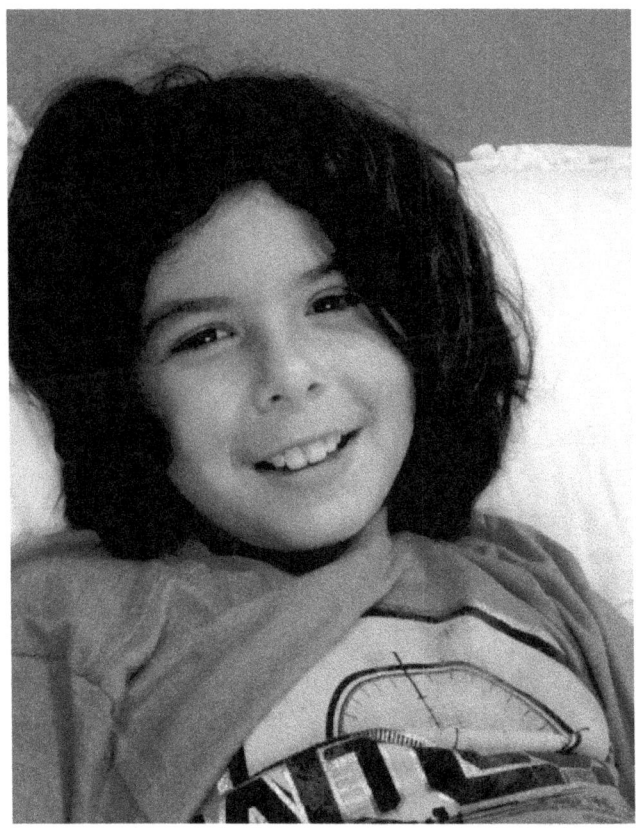

October 2012

In my family, we have a saying: "You don't know who your true friends are, until...." This was an "until" moment and it was amazing how many friends and family really stepped up to the plate for us. One of my best friends, Laurie, set up a meal train, and it was just the beginning of months of food (and more food and more food), flowers, treats, and gifts. Everyone just wanted to do everything and anything they could to help us.

Tanner's first round of chemotherapy was complete. Next up: going back into the hospital the following week to harvest his platelets in preparation for the stem cell treatment.

As I recount this, I remember that at that time, I did all I could do to keep Tanner occupied. I didn't know how it started, but when he was in the ICU, he would order things online...DVD's, videos, toys. He loved this, and it became his outlet. He became obsessed with DVD's and videos. He knew which ones he had and which ones he didn't have. The highlight of his day was waiting for his "deliveries" from the postman, UPS and Fed Ex trucks (buying from Amazon and eBay were daily musts). His favorites were DVD's and VHS tapes of his favorite cartoons: *SpongeBob*, *Blues Clues*, *Caillou*...the list went on.

As good as this was, as distracted as he was, there was a downfall. If the delivery didn't come when he was expecting it, he would get so mad. He would track each delivery and knew when it was supposed to arrive. When things didn't go according to plan, he would get extremely pissed off. Those moments were not fun...we liked when things went according to plan.

Tanner was not a spoiled child. Of course, like all good parents, we set limits. When it came to his online ordering, he didn't take advantage. Friends and family were always asking what they could send to Tanner. Gift cards were always the clear winner. The whole process of ordering and getting his deliveries, from beginning to end, was something he enjoyed. It was something that brought a smile to his face. I would rather he focus on that, than the reality of terminal brain cancer.

It was October, and one of our typical "clinic" days. Little did I know this "typical clinic day" would have a lasting impact.

Dr. T walked in and, right behind her, a social worker. I knew this was not a good sign. I was already sitting down, so they gave me the news. The very bad news.

Tanner tested positive for the mutant p53 gene.

Both Greg and I needed to get tested immediately. Most likely Tanner got the gene from one of us.

What does this mean? First, besides having a very high chance of getting cancer, no radiation was allowed. We were told, that when you have a mutated cancer gene, it is not advisable to have radiation, since it can cause additional cancer growth. Thank God we didn't do radiation.

I had my blood taken right then and there. Greg came in an hour later. It would take another month to get the results. All I can think was...we are fucked.

In the end of October, our good friends, the Cooper Family, organized a "Team Tanner" walk for the annual Brain Tumor Walk. They raised just under $14,000, and I was so amazed by the generosity and support of so many.

Greg and Casey would walk with our friends at the event. I wouldn't be there, as I would be at the hospital with Tanner as his platelets were harvested. A process called Pheresis, I learned.

It's a procedure that can only be done in the morning. A big machine takes the blood out of you, separates it, and then puts it back in. This was all in preparation for his stem cell transplant, the next step after chemotherapy, which we would do in February.

Pheresis sucked. Tanner hated it. I hated it. He had fits. Tantrums. The last place he wanted to be was there, back in the hospital. He missed home. He missed the mail. He missed my bed. He missed his cable and his TV shows. He hated being there and we all wanted him out as soon as possible. But it wasn't so simple. They could only take a certain amount of blood each day, and Dr. T wanted a particular amount harvested.

Finally, on October 31, I told her it was enough. We were so close to the goal, and it just wasn't worth his anxiety to stay one more night for a tiny bit more. We were going to go home...in time for Halloween.

Just before we were getting ready to leave, Tanner got a nosebleed. Tanner had always been a nosebleed kinda kid. Usually, we could handle it. This one, though, was bad. And it wouldn't stop. I was so scared that this nosebleed was a setback. It took an hour of doctors and nurses working to stop it before we were finally able to go home. We made it just before the sun set.

That Halloween, Tanner sat in a chair in front of the door and passed out candy. I had bought large size candy bars, and the kids knocking on our door were going crazy. They loved it.

We told each kid this was "Tanner's Candy Store" and everyone got a kick out of it.

As the night wore on, Tanner grew tired. After all, it had been a long few days. He cuddled with me on the couch and played with his iPad. It was good to be home.

November 2012

November. Birthday month. I always loved this month. It's Casey's birthday. It's Tanner's birthday. It's Thanksgiving. It's the kickoff to Christmas. Love this month... but this month, this year would be so different.

I truly couldn't believe this journey started two months ago. Being in the hospital for the stem cell transplant was so difficult. I was so glad it was over.

This month also kicked off cycle number two of chemotherapy. This time it would be outpatient. Two very long days in the clinic, but at the end of the day, we would be able to go home. Tanner tolerated the first round of chemotherapy pretty well, and we hoped for round two to be equally tolerable.

Despite his illness, Tanner was still the funny, loving, strong kid we all knew and loved. His life had changed dramatically - no school, no playing with friends, no going out. He would get tired and his appetite, on some days, was not what it used to be, but he was a trooper. As for Casey, she was the most incredible daughter and big sister. She was busy with dance, and school annoyed her like any eighth grader. Her life was different now, but she kept a smile on her face that brightened each and every day.

This was a whole new learning curve for me. With cancer, it was no longer one day at a time; it was one moment. We were told to always expect the unexpected.

Round two of chemotherapy brought a very long day in clinic and Tanner got through it like a champ. But then the unexpected happened, a fever in the middle of the night. So there we were, checking into the hospital once again. Tests done, chemotherapy finished, sleepless nights and finally we were back home… home sweet home.

Turns out Tanner had a virus, the simple virus that my kids have had through the years, except having a virus when you have cancer isn't so simple. Waking up that morning, in my own bed, with Tanner asleep next to me was simply the best. He was feeling better from his virus, but feeling kind of yucky from the chemotherapy. I was hoping for a quiet weekend with Tanner and Casey, a quiet week to come, but then again, I had to remember: it was one moment at a time.

We talked to Dr. T and decided that Tanner should have another MRI soon, instead of waiting until next month. He'd had two rounds of chemotherapy, and we all wanted to know what was happening and whether the treatment was working.

A glioblastoma is a very aggressive tumor. The way it had always been described to me is that it was like an octopus' tentacles intertwined with the brain. And although 100% of the tumor was removed in surgery, there were still those microscopic cells that the surgeons were unable to remove. It was one powerful tumor. You just hoped the treatment was strong enough to kill off all of those cells and for the tumor not to return.

On November 15, Tanner had his MRI. It was a nightmare. He had to be sedated, and he wouldn't let the nurses put in his IV. He fought. He lashed out. He was out of control. Finally the IV went in. We needed this MRI. We needed to see what was going on.

I remember sitting in the waiting room and talking to another mom. Her son was about three-years-old and had had cancer since he was an infant. Her son basically never had known a life without cancer. It made me so sad. Tanner had ten healthy years, but this little boy had had practically none. We both had sons that were different ages; we both had sons with different cancers. The one thing we did have in common was our children were both patients of Dr. T.

After the MRI, we went home. Dr. T was away at a conference. We asked that she be the one to give us the results. We didn't want the news from the doctor on call. We didn't want the news to come from a stranger. Having said that, we knew it meant that we would have to get through the weekend without knowing the results.

The day after the MRI was a Friday, a clinic day. As Tanner and I were sitting in the waiting room, a nurse, I had become friendly with, found me and started some small talk. I asked if they had the MRI results, just checking to make sure they received them. She asked me if I wanted to know the results. I explained it was not that we didn't want to know the results, it was that we didn't want to hear them from a "stranger doctor." We wanted to hear the results from someone we knew.

In a weird way, she kept pushing me to get the results from her. Something was telling me I wanted to hear what she had to say. So, I told her to tell me. And she did.

She told me the MRI showed the cancer was dead. At first, she used a medical word that I didn't know...necrosis. But then she used the word that I would understand... dead. The cancer was dead. The chemotherapy killed it. I started to cry. I hugged her. The tears would not stop. She told me she had wanted to call me at home last night to tell me the good news.

I asked to see the MRI report. She got the paperwork, and we walked into a room. As she held it in her hands, I looked at it, and I didn't see anything that resembled what she had just told me. Nothing. She then said that it must be an old report and she would find the latest one.

In the meantime, Tanner got his blood drawn. After the blood test, she asked me to come into another room, and she shut the door. There's that fucking shut door again. We know what that means.

She handed me the report, and I started to read it. It was the complete opposite from what she just said. She told me she was sorry, but she got us confused with another patient. These were our correct results. It was bad. The report confirmed that there was new growth. Just the opposite of death, it was the birth of the tumor. I left the office. I couldn't breathe.

I didn't know what to think. I tried to rationalize it. Maybe the report she showed me was the original MRI from September, and she got confused. We would know Monday for sure when Dr. T returned. Honestly, I didn't even want to think about it. It was so hard to digest this on my own, but I did. I went the entire weekend not telling anyone what had happened.

On November 19, we spent the whole day in clinic while Tanner got blood and platelets. Casey was with us. Dr. T was back in town. She asked someone to take Casey for a walk, so she could be alone with Greg and me. It couldn't be good. And I was right.

It was not. The tumor was growing. The worst news we could get. She showed us the report. It was the shitty report that I had already seen. I had to pretend I was getting this horrific news for the first time.

Tomorrow, Casey turns fourteen. How could her birthday even be normal? Never did I think that the start of November birthday celebrations would be like this. It was just too much. I needed to wake up from this terrible nightmare.

Later that evening, Tanner got a fever. We went back to the hospital. He ended up there for ten days…during Casey's birthday, his birthday and Thanksgiving. It would be the last birthday we would celebrate with him.

Everything had happened so fast and at once, that Greg and I really didn't have a chance to digest the bad news Dr. T had given us. I mean, we knew it, we heard it, but those first few days, we didn't have the chance to talk, really talk about it.

I finally told Greg and Michael what had happened with the nurse. One might ask, one might wonder, why didn't I do something, say something, in that moment? What happened was not okay. The answer is…I don't know. I'm a tough person. I speak my mind. I say it like it is. There's a part of me that wanted to scream at the nurse. But then there was that part that just felt defeated. Nothing I could say or do could change what was…that Tanner was sick and dying.

Rainbow Around The Son

On the flip side, I remembered one thing. Remember that mom I spoke to when Tanner had his MRI...the one whose son has had cancer since he was an infant? I like to think it was his MRI results that the nurse got confused with ours. That this little boy's cancer was gone, and he had a chance to finally, finally live healthy years. I will never know if this is what happened. I do know someone that day got good results. It wasn't us, but somewhere out there, a family was rejoicing. I hope that child is still okay and healthy.

We spent Thanksgiving in the hospital. We brought in our turkey dinner and ate it on paper plates. We were thankful to be together, to have Tanner with us. But we knew, in our hearts, that this would most likely be the last Thanksgiving we would spend with our son.

I did feel grateful for a lot...each moment that Tanner was happy and funny and silly and goofy and cuddly and loving; for the beauty, courage, dedication and love that is Casey; for Greg and his strength and patience, and for being an amazing Dad to the kids; for my wonderful family who has stood by us through this nightmare; for Michael, who loves me like no other, and had become an integral part of Tanner's life; and for my friends, who checked in on us daily to see what they could do to make any of our days just a little brighter.

On November 25, my baby boy turned eleven.

Ten terrible days later, we finally went home. We couldn't rest for even a minute, as we needed to make decisions about what to do next. I was truly living a nightmare.

Greg and I met privately with Dr. T the very next day. Her office had no windows, and I felt like there was no air. She told us: "The tumor is very aggressive and growing fast. Tanner could live for a few weeks to a few months."

We needed to make plans. We asked about other treatment options. Radiation? In a situation like this, even with a mutated gene, sometimes radiation trumps everything and is the temporary solution. Dr. T told us it would buy us a little time, maybe a few weeks. We also had to consider, with his radiation treatment, Tanner would have to be sedated every day for six weeks.

I did not want to pursue this option. For me, it was always quality over quantity. If Tanner had radiation, it would compromise his quality of life. He was happy. He still had his head of hair. He still laughed, played, joked and had a great appetite. I had to make sure Tanner stayed this way.

Greg and I disagreed on what to do next. Greg wanted to do anything and everything. I didn't blame him. Of course, he would want that. All parents would. I would have done anything to save Tanner, but I was also looking at the big picture. Tanner was a different kind of kid. He was not the kind of kid who would have been okay with traveling the world for a cure. He was happiest at home. In my bed. On our couch. At our kitchen table. That's where he had to be.

Greg and I met with our therapist. Greg wanted to do the radiation. I knew that just to get "a few more weeks" was not worth the damage it could do. Greg simply didn't want to give up. Neither did I, but I knew in my gut, in my heart of hearts, we could not do radiation.

Several months earlier, when Tanner was first diagnosed, I had a conversation with my hairdresser, Kimberley. Many years ago, her husband died of a glioblastoma. I asked her, if she could go back and do anything different, what would it be? She said no radiation. The radiation changed him. It was the one mistake she made. I kept that with me. I remembered that.

I fought hard against it with Greg. Our therapist sided with me. And in the end, Greg relented. He was sad, but knew it was the right thing to do for Tanner. We knew we had to make every day be the best. Time was not on our side.

The end result? We stopped treatment. No more chemotherapy. No radiation. We would try oral chemotherapy, which we could give to him at home, as long as he could tolerate it. Quality over quantity.

On top of everything else that was happening to our family, we were given more terrible news.

Greg tested positive for the mutant p53 gene.

I was negative. Tanner inherited it from him. We knew the next step was to test Casey. There was no choice.

December 2012

Everything was different now. Now that we knew Tanner's cancer was growing. Now that we knew it was "weeks to months." My dad came over every day. My mom hadn't been feeling well, so she would come by when she could. We all knew time was not on our side. We just hoped and prayed for a miracle, and for the clock to tick very, very slowly.

Last month, when we were in the hospital, it just sucked...it was brutal. The hardest part was that after the first few days, Tanner felt fine, since his fever went away. But his blood work wasn't normal, and because his white cell count wasn't high enough for him to go home (he was neutropenic), they kept him in the hospital longer.

I had to keep Tanner busy. I had to keep him occupied and distracted. One night, when it was late, I got the idea to look at cars online. I was a minivan-driving Mom for a long time, but with the kids now older, I had finally graduated and didn't need a minivan anymore.

All Tanner wanted was for me to get another minivan. He had one in mind: a Dodge Caravan. I don't know why, but that's the minivan he wanted me to get. One late night we went online and "designed" a van...complete with a DVD player. He thought it was that simple...that you designed one and got it. I told him that it was not something you put in the shopping cart, and it gets shipped out the next day. Or was it?

The timing actually worked. My lease was ending, and I needed to get a new car. A minivan (again?!) was not my obvious first choice, but the things we do for our kids...right? I knew someone who knew someone who owned a Dodge dealership. I am not a favor-asking kind of person, but I needed help. I talked to someone and explained what was going on. He was able to get me a good deal and a short term lease on a minivan. So, we surprised Tanner, and once again we were a minivan-driving family.

Every day, every moment, I was with Tanner. And I could now get him out more in the new minivan. One day I asked him, if you could go anywhere, any place, that you have never been, where would you want to go? His answer, "Walmart." And so, we went.

One day my mom came over to visit, and we decided to let Tanner "drive" the minivan. He would never live to drive a car on his own, so this was the next best thing we could do for him. With my mom and Casey in the car, I put Tanner on my lap. I controlled the pedals, and he guided the steering wheel (with my help of course). We drove around the neighborhood, and Casey filmed him on her phone. He was so happy! Tanner would ask which way to go, "Left, right or straight?" We only drove for a little while... just long enough to create an incredible memory.

As the days flew by, all I wanted to do was breathe him in. His laughter. His smile. His frustration. We talked, we cuddled, we hugged, we kissed. I took pictures and videos constantly. I wanted to remember every second with both of my kids. Even though I knew the inevitable, it still was incomprehensible that this was my reality.

We were told we could reach out to Make-A-Wish and Tanner could be granted a wish. We talked with him and tried to find a wish that would work best. We suggested he spend a day with the crew of *Jackass,* since he loved those movies and thought the stunts they did were the funniest ever. Not really appropriate for an eleven-year-old, though. So we thought again. Maybe something with the show *Diners, Drive-Ins and Dives,* since he watched it all the time? Or what about getting his own skill crane? He loved those arcade claw machines, where you win a stuffed animal, and he was always very good at it.

And so that was the wish that was granted...he was given an arcade size skill crane machine, filled with stuffed animals, that now sat in our family room. It made him smile and happy and distracted. We all had fun with it.

Christmas was coming. Although we are Jewish, we had always celebrated Christmas. More so than Hanukkah. It was a holiday that both Tanner and Casey loved. About a week or so before Christmas, I went with Casey to get a tree. A small one. Tanner wanted nothing to do with it. In fact, before we could even decorate it, he put it on its side and dragged it out the front door. I left the tree outside in our courtyard. Tanner informed us that he didn't want Christmas this year. No presents. No nothing.

We respected his wishes.

On December 24, Tanner woke up with Christmas excitement. "What's Santa bringing me?" What? Now he wanted Christmas? I should have known he would change his mind. I should have been prepared. We moved the Christmas tree back inside the house.

I called my dad and got his help. I asked him to run to the mall and get anything he thought Tanner would want. I ran to CVS and bought Lotto scratchers, gift cards and just silly junky stuff. Last minute Christmas was definitely going to happen at our home.

That night, Casey and Tanner hung out in her room. They didn't fall asleep until way after midnight. They sat in her bed, each with their own computers and played *Toon Town*, a silly computer game that they loved to do together. I watched them. Taking it all in. "Remember this." They ended up in my bed. I watched them sleep. I etched this moment in my heart forever.

Christmas morning. They woke up together, as they always had done and tip toed down the stairs to see if Santa had come. It was their tradition. We made it a happy day. A Merry Christmas, of course.

Those days between Christmas and New Year's Eve were sad. Bittersweet. We knew this Christmas would be his last one. We approached New Year's knowing it would be his last one.

One night I couldn't sleep…even more than usual. My mind was racing with so many questions. Dreaded questions that seemed (somewhat) logical when you were told your son was going to die. I needed to be honest with myself so I wrote down each question, each fear. As hard as it was, it was something I had to do:

1. *How does it go from being normal (like how everything is okay with him) to a decline?*

2. *What can I expect during the decline?*

3. *What symptoms will I see? Seizures? Headaches?*

4. *Will he be conscious?*

5. *At what point does he become unconscious?*

6. *Is it true the hearing is the last to go?*

7. *Will he still hear my words or feel my touch if he is unconscious?*

8. *How does he go to the bathroom? Will he need diapers?*

9. *How will I know when it is the end?*

10. *What happens when death happens?*

11. *What will I see?*

12. *Will there be a death rattle?*

13. *Will it be scary? Or is it peaceful?*

14. *Does anything happen to the body once it dies? Does it go to the bathroom? Is there blood?*

15. *What will he feel like? Will he be cold?*

16. *Does it smell?*

17. *How do I hold/touch/feel/kiss a dead body?*

18. *Who should be in the room?*

19. *We will ask Casey what she wants, but how can she handle it if we can hardly handle it?*

20. *How much time is the right time to be with the body before it's time to let it go?*

21. *How do they get his body to the mortuary?*

22. *How do we get his body out of the house?*

23. *Will the neighbors see?*

24. *Do we carry him or do they take him? Is he covered?*

25. *What happens at the mortuary?*

26. *Is it true a member of the family has to confirm it is his body before the funeral?*

27. *How do I handle having his body go into the ground?*

28. *How do I handle being away from him?*

29. *He hates the dark. He is scared without me. How do I let him go knowing these things?*

30. *How do I leave the cemetery knowing he's there all alone?*

31. *Who protects him now?*

32. *Who will help him?*

33. *Who will comfort him?*

34. *He's so dependent on me...*

35. *How do I go on?*

36. *How do I go day by day?*

37. *How do I function?*

38. *How do I go on with life?*

39. *How do I find my new normal?*

40. *How do I find myself going back out? Enjoying a glass of wine with friends? How do I do that?*

41. *Will he contact me?*

42. *Do we tell him what's going on?*

43. *When do we tell him what's going on?*

44. *If he's scared now, and a part of him doesn't know, how scared will he be when he knows?*

45. *How do I forgive those who are not there for me (friends and family)?*

46. *How do I let go of my anger?*

47. *How do I deal with those who want to see him for their own satisfaction (people Tanner doesn't even know)?*

48. *How do I believe again?*

49. *What is my purpose?*

50. *How do I deal with those who do reach out and I have anger/issues with?*

51. *How do I deal with those who haven't reached out who should have?*

52. *How is it that he seems so fine now...it's like a cruel joke is being played on us.*

53. *I keep going back to the thought that I'm scared for him... afterwards. Who will take care of him? Love him like I do? Comfort him like I do? Protect him from things he's scared of like the rain, the dark, fireworks and thunderstorms? Will he be mad at me? Angry at me? Will he be like he is now or in Heaven will he be a kid with no issues, strong and independent?*

54. *He doesn't know...it breaks my heart.*

December 31. New Year's Eve and also my dad's birthday. Both Greg and Michael came over, and we rang in the New Year as a family. We sat on our stairs and watched the living room television broadcast the ball drop. Tanner counted down. I watched him say the numbers. I recorded him. Another moment etched in my heart. Tears rolled down my face, because I knew this would be the last time I would ever see this, the last time he would ever do this. Short of a miracle, we knew he would not live to countdown the year again...2013 would be his last.

January 2013

With the New Year, I decided to start writing everything down...journaling it all daily. The good. The bad. The important stuff. The not so important stuff. In the end, though, all of it was important, because every day with Tanner was a day we didn't expect. We were on borrowed time.

1.1.13

Day one of the new year. A day to be enjoyed. A day to start fresh. A renewal. The day to start the diet. The day to exercise. The day to call a friend or family member. What is this day to me? A reminder of the beginning of what was to come. The sadness. The shock. The anticipation of the worst thing ever.

So, as I went into 2013...which would be the saddest year ever, I promised myself I would remember the good in each day. Because I didn't know when the bad would come.

Today, Tanner was happy, happy, happy. Greg made pancakes, and Tanner wanted more and more because he was a "big boy." He smiled and laughed. He helped Greg fold laundry and wanted to sweep the floors. He made the best of today.

I took advantage of Tanner's good day and went down to the beach...just to get away for a few minutes. Feel the air. The sunshine. The ocean breeze. The beauty. For a quick minute, I forgot it all.

That night, Tanner helped serve dinner to Casey and me. Although he didn't want his dinner (he said he was full), he devoured the Krispy Kreme donuts that we had bought earlier. He and Casey baked a cake...his idea. Her idea was to make two layers...one red and one purple, their favorite colors.

I thought back to the past year. I couldn't help it. It was what we all do on New Year's, right? How it all changed for us on that September day. I thought back to the end of November, when Dr. T met with us in her office and told us, "it's not good." She told us to "make plans." She told us it could be "weeks to months." Here we were in 2013...a year I wasn't sure he would live to see...but here we were.

Entering this New Year, I looked at myself and all that had happened so far. My strength, my endurance, my will, my priorities. I had already learned more...seen more...than many people will ever see in a lifetime. My life was with Tanner and my family. I spent every waking moment with Tanner. Any moments that I could escape for dinner, I went out with Michael. I didn't see most of my friends anymore, because honestly, Tanner wanted me to himself. There were a few friends that I allowed into my inner circle. A few of my closest girlfriends. A few of my closest guy friends.

With the New Year, I had also been thinking a lot about Tanner, not just focusing on his illness, but about the "before."

Tanner wasn't an easy kid. He had special needs. Or as my dad has said...he didn't have special needs...he was special. He was this different sort of kid.

When he was a baby, he was so good. Much better than Casey. I remember once he was taking a nap in his crib. Casey never even used her crib. She was in our bed...always. I remember turning to my mom and saying that I thought something might be wrong with Tanner. She said, "No. He's just a good baby. You're not used to that." How true it was. But then it changed. Casey went from being a tough baby to truly a perfect little girl. Tanner, just the opposite. Great baby. Tough, tough kid.

We knew Tanner had some delays. At the age of two and a half he wasn't talking much. He did everything else on time...it was the talking that was the issue. We weren't that concerned, but still, as proactive as we were, we needed to find out what was going on.

That was just the beginning. Lack of speech equaled lack of communication, which equaled frustration and some behavior issues. It was like a domino effect. He ended up in speech therapy, occupational therapy and social skills. We met with doctor upon doctor upon doctor. He could not be labeled. It wasn't Autism. It wasn't Asperger's. It was that "grey" area. Developmental delay was all they could call it. We were hopeful this was something he would one day outgrow.

Life was not easy with him. Many sacrifices were made from all of us. We would go to a restaurant, a movie, a mall, even Disneyland, and suddenly he didn't want to be there anymore. Many times we had to leave. His tantrums and outbursts just weren't worth staying somewhere, where he would make it miserable.

I remember once we were at a restaurant. A restaurant that we went to all the time. A place where he felt comfortable and safe. But one particular Saturday, he wasn't feeling it. He was younger, I don't know, maybe four or five years old. I don't remember the circumstances or why, but he was having a bad day. I took him out of the restaurant and while outside, he hit me and lashed out at me.

Rainbow Around The Son

As this was happening, some lady who had been in the restaurant came outside. She had been staring at us inside…not a nice stare. I didn't know her. I was at my wit's end and frustrated. She gave me a dirty look and said something rude to me. I couldn't believe it. I remember saying, "What's your problem?" She told me I was a terrible mom because I let my son hit me. A terrible mom. That was the wrong thing to say to me. So I gave it to her. I just told her off.

I was so angry. Here was this stranger who lashed out judgment at a situation she knew nothing about. She had no idea what was going on. Kids aren't perfect. Issues or not, kids have bad moments. Be empathetic; not judgmental. Be kind and never judge a book by its cover.

On the flip side, Tanner was the most loving, funny, smart, sweet kid. He had a smile that just rocked your world. He had this look in his eyes that would melt your heart. A great personality with great comedic timing. He made people laugh. He made an impression on people. His love, affection and humor were his saving grace. Many, including his teachers, would forget about his behavioral issues, because he would just win them over with his smile. He was like no other.

Now that he was sick, I thought his differences were, in a way, saving him. He didn't know on a daily basis, on an hourly basis, what he was up against; he was able to just be himself. To be a kid. To live. All he wanted was to not be in school. To do what he wanted to do, and to be with me. And he got that. Every single day (except for hospital and clinic visits). No pressure. No expectations. No homework. No responsibilities. He just lived.

1.2.13

The day started at 1:15 a.m. I fell asleep, but then woke up to find Tanner still awake. He showed me that there was a new *Peppa Pig* show available, and then his tears started. It had happened before…he would start to cry and just needed me to hold him. To tell him it was okay. I did just that. I loved him. I loved him more than any words can ever say. I comforted him. We held each other. I told him stories and about how lucky I am to be his mom. I told him how he makes me laugh…how special he is to me…and to everyone else. I told him he's my blessing. My angel. My everything. I told him I will always be with him. I tried to tell him about the day he was born, but he didn't want to hear about it. He finally fell asleep.

Today we hung out at home and then went out later to CVS. Tanner "played" scratchers and it just wasn't a winning day. After winning only four dollars, I finally told him it was time to stop. A second later, I said, "Do you want to play one more?" He said yes and won $100. His face was priceless. It was frozen. He couldn't believe it. $100!!! He said to me, "My heart is happy."

Tonight, we talked about my birthday, which is on Friday, and what we should do. A visit to Walmart was the plan.

1.3.13

Pretty good day...hung out. Tanner had his blood test and Pentamidine (which was long overdue).

Pentamidine is an intravenous medicine Tanner had to take once a month. It was to prevent him from getting pneumonia, which can be so dangerous to a compromised immune system. For Tanner, it was not fun to do. It just meant a long time in clinic. We didn't like long visits.

Later that night, Tanner went to Michael's home without me, to hang out with his girls and play Wii. At first, I was upset, scared, nervous for him to be somewhere where I wasn't. I had to take Casey to dance and would be across town, in traffic. A blessing in disguise. He had the best time...created memories with Michael, Katie and Emily. So happy he felt able to do it.

Kisses at midnight for my birthday...nothing better.

1.4.13

My birthday...today I am forty-two. We went to Walmart. And Toys "R" Us. And In-N-Out. Just the typical places a Mama wants to go to on her birthday...lol. We got back home, and Casey and my dad went out. They came back with a cake, balloons, flowers, cards and presents. Tanner made me a card (thanks to Casey's help) and we made wishes on my birthday candles and blew them out. I was sure we all made the same wish.

Then, all of a sudden, my life changed...once again.

My mom was diagnosed with leukemia. AML. She told me today...on my birthday.

She goes into the hospital next week for one month. Thankfully, the doctors found it early and the prognosis was good, but the treatment is difficult...very difficult. I couldn't even help her. I would be helping Tanner. I was scared for her. Scared for me. Scared for Casey. Scared for Tanner.

It was just too much. All of it. My family was healthy, and now another cancer? What the fuck? I knew this was not about me - but, honestly, it was about me...it affects my family, my life. A weight of a million pounds on my shoulders. I was just so scared and tired of it all. Happy fucking birthday to me.

1.5.13

Another good day with Tanner. Greg got us into an advanced screening of *Despicable Me 2*. It comes out in July, but, well, you know...we didn't know where we would be in July. We drove out to Thousand Oaks, and Tanner lasted ten minutes in the movie. He didn't want to see it. He said we weren't supposed to see a movie that was not supposed to come out until the summer. He was so funny like that. So, we left.

1.6.13

My mom and my stepdad Stan came over for breakfast. My brother Grant, Greg and Michael were here, too. I told my mom to be strong...to fight this. What else could I say? I told her that in the past few months with Tanner, I had come to know well this very difficult road we were on, a road where we had few choices and even less control. There will be days she will want to give up, but she can't. Even in the lowest moments, she can't give up. Even when things get bad here with Tanner, and she can't be here, she has to fight. We would take care of Tanner. She needed to take care of herself and get better. She could beat this.

1.7.13

The holidays were over and Casey went back to school today. Tanner will miss not having her around 24/7. Watching them play was one of my biggest joys. Being goofy and making each other laugh...no greater pleasure.

Tanner woke up with a big smile and so much energy. It really doesn't make sense. How can someone have his diagnosis and be so alive and seemingly healthy?

"Anyone can give up, it's the easiest thing in the world to do. But to hold it together when everyone else would understand if you fell apart, that's true strength."- A quote I found that so rings true for me.

Every day I was doing my best...it was just so hard.

1.8.13

I watched Tanner sleep. I made sure one of my body parts was always touching one of his. It was usually my feet to his. Sometimes I would put my hand on his hip. Just to feel him there.

Each morning I held my breath...waiting for him to wake up. Waiting for his smile, his asking for the computer, his checking the weather and his emails and what deliveries were coming today. His asking if the fireplace was on downstairs. His grabbing my computer and running down the stairs...and so another day started.

1.9.13

Now that the holidays had passed, we knew we had to deal with testing Casey for the mutant p53 gene. I scheduled an appointment for next week with the genetic department and Dr. T. Casey will have her blood taken then to test for the mutant p53 gene.

1.10.13

Dr. T had suggested bringing in hospice for Tanner. So, we did. At first, they really weren't doing anything with him, but we wanted them active in our lives for when that "just in case" moment happened. They gave us an emergency kit that we kept in the refrigerator. All I knew was that it had morphine in it. They weighed him, they talked to him, they talked to me.

1.11.13

I sat and watched Tanner. Stared at him. Memorized him. His little nose. His lips. His eyes. His cheeks. I watched him watch TV. I watched him on the computer. Memorizing each breath in, each breath out. His expressions. His eyes movements. He always took everything in. He watched TV while he was on the computer. That was his thing. To do many things at once. To be focused on one thing, but always knowing what was going on in the background.

I took Casey to dinner. Just the two of us. We sat down and enjoyed our meal. Two men sat down next to us…older men. Casey and I were engaged in a conversation, and tears welled up. The man next to me interrupted and made a comment about child rearing. He assumed our conversation and tears were about typical teenage mishaps and bad behavior. He told me he "killed" his three kids. "How?" I asked. He said he gave one too much love, and the other two, not enough. Very telling. I politely explained the meaning behind our tears and conversation. His already white hair seemed to turn even whiter, when he heard about Tanner. He was incredibly apologetic and embarrassed. He apologized for interrupting our meal, and said he never should have talked to us. I told him it was okay. He picked up our bill…paid for our whole dinner.

1.12.13

Long day. Casey had dance all afternoon. I took Tanner to the mall. After some time walking around we left, and he just didn't know what he wanted to do. Frustration. We drove around, stopped at a few places, and he ended up guiding me to Pet Smart. I bought him a hamster. Made him so happy. That's all I cared about.

I picked up Casey. She wanted a hamster, too. I was consciously trying to make sure she didn't feel left out. The center of our world was Tanner, as we tried to make up for every second of the now, knowing it was so short. We went back and got her one. Tanner named his Elephant. She named hers Dash.

Later that night, Casey accidently spilled water on my computer. I got upset. Yelled at the kids. Got angry. The fear of losing everything on here...my work, my writing, but more importantly my pictures. My videos. Everything of my kids. Of Tanner. I apologized for yelling...and I backed up my computer.

1.13.13

Greg spent the day here, and I took a few hours to myself. Later on, Michael and I went to dinner. A belated birthday dinner for me. We shared food, champagne, gimlets, espresso and baileys. A very much needed night.

1.14.13

Greg had surgery on his foot today. Tanner and I picked him up. Several times, in the car, Tanner said out loud, "Let go of me." I asked him about it. What did that mean? Who was he talking to? He didn't answer me.

1.16.13

Today was a clinic day. Not the usual kind, though. Yes, Tanner was getting blood taken, but the main purpose was to get Casey tested for the mutant p53. I prayed (not sure who I pray to anymore, though) that she didn't have it. We would know in the next few weeks.

Tanner held Casey's hand as the nurse took her blood. I watched my babies…blood being taken…hands held…how did we get here?

When we got back home, Tanner was a little off. Seemed tired. Not his usual vibrant self. As for me? I had such a fear in the back of my mind. "Please let her test be negative." The thought was overwhelming.

1.17.13

At 3 a.m. Tanner started to stir. He wasn't feeling well. He threw up. He mentioned something about his head, but dismissed it. He wanted me to hold my hand on his head. That reminded me of the week before he was diagnosed. He had me do the same thing. He finally fell back asleep.

He woke up tired and said that he couldn't go outside, because of his head. He didn't complain that it hurt, so I didn't know if he was scared to tell me, or if it was a different kind of hurt. He was very clingy and tired that morning. Finally at around 10:30 a.m. he started to brighten up.

Casey was upset today. School, life, Tanner…everything was overwhelming. I felt so bad. I wished I could make it all okay. For her. For Tanner. For me. For my mom. For all of us. But it was all out of my control. I had never felt such sadness. At least not yet.

1.18.13

Tanner made Valentines for his class. He did them a month early, because, well, you know. I asked if we could go to school to visit his teachers and friends. "No," he said. So I mailed them.

It was a hard day…he didn't know what he wanted. At first, he wanted me next to him. Then he didn't want me in the room. Later on, he got very upset…crying. "Am I ok?" he asked me. When he does this, I get so scared. I think these are the moments that he knows something is really wrong. And it's not that he shouldn't know the truth, the reality. He should know. He does know.

1.19.13

I broke up with Michael today. He is so great…this whole situation is just so complicated. He's here for me, yet he has his life too. And honestly, I feel so alone. We love each other... it's just so hard.

My relationship with Michael had never been easy. We met at the wrong time...well, maybe it was the right time, but maybe it wasn't. For various reasons, our relationship had a faulty start. We were friends for many months before we became more than just friends. And then, when our relationship really started, really took off, Tanner got sick.

Relationships are never easy, and it certainly wasn't easy to be in a relationship, when you're dealing with illness and a terminally ill child. We have had our ups and downs, many ups and downs. I needed him by my side. He needed me.

As usual, our breakup didn't last long. Maybe a few hours. We loved each other too much for it to last longer.

1.20.13

I dreamt last night that we were doing euthanasia on Tanner. WTF?

Casey bought film for her Polaroid camera, and tonight's activity was taking pictures. Tanner loved it. We went through rolls of film. We took very cute pictures. I loved creating memories like this.

Today I shared something with my dad. I will have no regrets. None. I have been the best Mom to Tanner. I said "I love you" to him one hundred times a day...he was probably sick of it. I kissed him and hugged him and touched him and cuddled with him and scratched his back and put my hand on his side and told him how amazing and incredible he was, and how I would always be with him – always and how lucky I was to be his Mom, and how happy he made me, and how very much I loved him. I did all that over and over and over every single day. He knew. He would always know. I would never be the person to think that I didn't say it enough. I could say that I wish I could still do those things, but I would never say that I didn't do it enough.

1.21.13

Dr. T had suggested doing another MRI. The last one we had was in November, and it was the one that gave us the grim diagnosis. Greg wanted do another one. I did not. Dr. T had it scheduled for Thursday. I just didn't want to do it. It was just going to be bad news. I was sure of it. I couldn't handle another test where it said how bad it was. That happened to us last time. What was the point? We knew what was going on. Yes, it was happening more slowly than we thought, but there was no miracle. If there were a miracle, then a year from now we could do the MRI. I didn't want to have to put him through the stress of it. Going to the hospital. Knocking him out with Propofol. Having him wake up. Being told bad news once again.

I was so scared. I love this boy more than anything in the world. I watched him through the corner of my eye. I took note of everything. He was watching *Barney* on the computer, and *Team Umizoomi* was on the TV. He was eating a Cherry Airheads popsicle on my chair. We were both breathing. Sharing the same air. We were several feet away from each other. We were together. How in the world would I one day not have days like this? He was my breath. My love. My life. My baby.

Tonight, after Tanner had his bath, he came up to me and said, "Look at my pimples." Tanner had had pimples on his face, since the start of his illness. For the first time, in a long time, they were going away. I told him, "The pimples are all gone." He said, "Yeah, I'm better now. Am I better?" He was equating his pimples with being better. What do you say to that?

1.22.13

After we decided to stop treatment, we were given the option to give him oral chemotherapy, Etoposide. The side effects are very minimal, if any. It was just a pill he would take at home every day. So that's what we did. We would try it as long as he tolerated it. And so far, it had been fine.

Rainbow Around The Son

As the week crept by, the looming MRI appointment came closer. This MRI thing was just so upsetting to me. There was a question if we should think about giving him a different treatment (Avastin), so the MRI would help us in making that decision. The oral chemotherapy he was taking seemed to be okay. So, what was the point in changing things? If it's not broke, why fix it? Things had been mostly status quo, except I did notice some decline in the past week. I didn't want to put him through the stress of an MRI and change treatment and perhaps something worse could happen. At the end of the day, this cannot be fixed. I just didn't know what to do.

I forgot what I did, but at some point, Tanner looked at me and said, "You're my hero." It was over something silly, like getting him a yogurt or something, but he told me I'm his hero. That just blew me away. Me, his hero? He's my hero.

Tonight, Tanner watched this *Blue Clues* show called *Blue's Big Musical Movie*. At the end of the show, there was the big song that said, "You can be anything that you want to be." The kids used to sing it all the time. After the song, Tanner got very emotional. Crying. He told me it made him sad. He was hysterical. He said, "It hurts my heart." He was heartbroken. He then said, several times, "Mommy, I am dying." Dying. He used that word. Dying. I was devastated. Casey heard it too and ran into my room. "He didn't say what I think he just said?" she asked me. "Yes, you heard it right," I answered. I put my hand over his heart and comforted him.

Later that night Casey wanted to sleep in bed with us. He didn't want her in my bed. I felt so bad. She ended up going back into her room. I had to give into him. My baby. He said he was dying. This was just too much. I would never forget this moment. And I haven't.

1.23.13

Tanner woke up with a smile on his face, but stayed upstairs all day. It was because of the clouds. The weather. Not because he was not strong enough to go downstairs. He went up and down several times, in fact. He just didn't want to see the clouds.

I talked to him about doing the MRI again. He said, "No, Mommy I can't. It's not good. It will make my brain bleed. There will be blood on my brain." Where does a kid come up with this? I voted for no MRI. Maybe in time, but not now. The decision had been made.

1.24.13

It was Thursday and raining. The day he was supposed to have his MRI. Except we were not. Home all day. A very good day.

Tanner loved his DVD's and VHS tapes. Since he became sick, though, he discovered the world of his favorite shows shown in different countries. I had no idea where he discovered this, but that was Tanner for you. He would go onto iTunes and find the shows, but apparently people in the USA can't have iTunes Australia. A concept he was very pissed off about. I don't blame him.

A fight to take his medicine, but he did it. He didn't go to bed until 1:30 a.m.

1.25.13

Raining again. We went in for a blood test. Not much of a fight. A quick in and out. Wish it was always like that.

Greg and I had an argument. Greg thought we should put a contingency plan in place. "What if this goes on for years?" he asked. He felt we couldn't keep going on like this every day... normalcy needed to come back. Years? Years? It's only been a few months. Let's get to a year and then talk contingency plans.

1.26.13

Michael told me about a dream he had. It blew me away.

Michael saw a little boy. It took him a minute to realize it was Tanner. It was the way Tanner looked at Casey's Bat Mitzvah, but an older version. He was still short, it was definitely him, just a little older, maybe thirteen or fourteen.

Tanner approached Michael and looked him in the eyes. He took his hands and told Michael, "Tell my mom I'm okay and not to worry." Michael asked him why he couldn't tell me himself. Tanner said he couldn't because he was still alive and he couldn't tell me that while he was still alive. Tanner was fine. No speech issue. Not sick. He was totally fine.

It was future Tanner talking to Michael today. Completely blew me away. I wanted Michael to write it down exactly as he remembered it.

1.27.13

Sunday. We slept until a little after 10 a.m. Greg made breakfast. I went to visit my mom at the hospital. First time I saw her. It was hard to go to that hospital. Brought back so many memories of Tanner's surgery. It used to be a "good" hospital to me. Happy memories. Memories of giving birth to both Casey and Tanner. Now it just scared me. My mom seemed to be doing better...grateful for that.

1.29.13

Tanner continued to amaze me. His happiness. His strength. He had no stress. No school. No expectations. He was just happy-go-lucky. This was why he was so strong. That was why he was still here.

February 2013

Blood and Pentamidine today. A little resistance, but he did great. Dr. T said he was doing amazing. Just amazing. I asked her whether a kid with a GBM and with a tumor such as his, with this type of growth - is this where she thought he would be? "No," she said. "No." He had gone above and beyond our expectations. Whatever we were doing, we were doing right. The Etoposide, the oral chemotherapy, was slowing this down and making his life good. Happy. Stress-free. Quality vs. quantity. He was an example to us all. Mind over matter.

Dr. T called this afternoon and reported that his blood count numbers were great, meaning they were not worse. They really had not changed much. She said he may not even need to come in once a week for blood. Maybe we can spread it out more? We would start round three of Etoposide on Sunday. Please let this continue. Things were good.

I took Casey to her dance party tonight and had dinner with Michael. I planned to sleep at his place, just to get away for one night, but I couldn't. I came home a little after midnight. I needed Tanner. I needed to be with him. He was so cuddly and clingy and cute. He told me, "I was worried about you."

2.2.13

Our lives had become Groundhog Day. Same thing...day in...day out...totally fine by me. Back in November, we were told time was not on our side. We were told to make "plans." We were told to prepare.

Here we were today...Groundhog Day. And we were blessed.

We stopped the aggressive treatment and opted for a treatment that was less aggressive and more doable for Tanner. We were told our new treatment, the oral chemotherapy, would merely slow things down and buy us a little time. What it had done, and continued to do, is make a boy happy and not feel sick. It had allowed him to go out and explore and do his thing at home (no more hospitals!)...he simply was enjoying his life.

The harsh reality, though, was that the prognosis was the same, and the end result would be the same. Our lives would forever be changed, but we were living for today, for the moment. This was a game changer, but as of now, the rules had not applied to our little guy. We had fun every day. We lived each day to its fullest with laughter, hugs and kisses.

February would be the month of celebration. We celebrated Tanner, as we always did, each and every moment. We celebrated Casey, who would be competing with 8 Count, her dance company team, at Showstoppers at the Disneyland Hotel...something we had been looking forward to for months. We celebrated my mom who would be coming home in a week, after a very tough month of treatment.

We were not out of the woods. We were merely on cruise control.

Tanner says to me:

"I just want to have you."

I say:

"You always have me."

He says:

"Always, Mommy?"

I say:

"Always, Tanner."

2.3.13

Super Bowl Sunday. 49ers versus Ravens.

Third cycle of Etoposide starts tonight...the oral chemotherapy wonder drug.

2.5.13

You know how there are moments in life that you remember above all? Good or bad...memories that just stay with you?

The phone rang. From my caller ID, I knew it was the hospital. I answered; it was the genetics doctor. A doctor I didn't even really know...we had only met once, actually.

This doctor told me the news over the phone.

Casey tested positive for the mutant p53 gene.

It took me a minute. I couldn't answer. That fucking cancer gene. I had the doctor repeat the news. I just didn't believe it. My world was turned upside down all over again.

I hung up the phone in a daze. Completely blindsided by what I was just told. I couldn't accept it as true, but it was.

I fell to the ground and just cried. I was truly defeated. And now I had to tell Casey that she had an over 90% chance of getting cancer.

I called Greg and told him the news. Silence. Devastation. Neither of us had the words.

Together, that evening, we told Casey. She took it so well. "It's not great, but I don't have cancer," she told us.

I no longer felt strong. I felt beaten. We had to get scans to make sure she was okay. What the fuck was going on here? WHAT THE FUCK?!

And so, our lives took another turn that day. It was no longer just about Tanner. It was now also about Casey…and keeping her healthy.

That was a huge turning point for us. Yes, Greg carried the gene, and of course, we would have to make sure he was okay. But it was different knowing your child had it. Your healthy child. We knew it was too late for Tanner. He had developed a cancer, from which you cannot recover. We couldn't save him. But with Casey we had a chance. As long as her initial, baseline scans showed her to be healthy, we would do everything in our power to keep her that way.

We decided to keep this information confidential. Our immediate family knew, of course, but it was not something we wanted to broadcast. It was important for people not to associate Casey having this mutant gene with Tanner having terminal cancer. There would be a time, and a place, when we would share this information. Just not now.

2.7.13

It was not only just about Tanner. It was also about Casey. I thought about her constantly. It was my mission. It was what I was now supposed to do with my life…to help find a cure for this mutant p53 gene. I needed to know that Casey was okay. I would not be able to save Tanner. I must save Casey.

I always knew we had to do something to make a difference. I knew when the time came, after Tanner passed away, we would do something to honor him. My dad and I had discussed that. So, after Casey's diagnosis we knew that whatever else we did, my dad and I would make it our life's mission about the mutant p53 gene. To save Casey. And others.

Tonight, I took Casey out of dance early. We met my dad at Restoration Hardware. We shopped for her room. The teenage redesign she had been wanting. We were doing it now. There was no more "waiting." She was happy.

2.8.13

Tanner wouldn't go to clinic today for blood. Dr. T said it was okay. His labs had been stable, so he could skip today.

Dr. T would be overseeing everything with Casey. She would need an MRI once a year…actually two MRI's…one for her brain and one for her whole body. Blood and urine tests every four months. Ultrasounds of her abdomen and pelvis every four months. I told Dr. T we needed to start this...now. I needed to make sure Casey was healthy. To have some kind of control over the health of my daughter, since I had none over my son.

The three of us stayed home tonight...me and my kids. We were goofy. We laughed and played. This is how it should always be.

2.12.13

Casey just met Lana del Rey, the highlight of our day. She was just hanging out in town and we spotted her, as did some other kids. I had never met a musician/celebrity quite like her. She was kind, genuine and real...and spent time with each kid, posed for pictures and signed autographs. We told her about Tanner, and she said she would include him in her prayers. What a true class act. Casey was always a big fan of hers. Now I am, too.

2.14.13

Valentine's Day. Tanner asked me to be his Valentine and for Valentine cuddles.

We needed to get hamster food, so we went to Pet Smart. While there, Tanner saw the dog tag machine and got the idea to make dog tags for everyone in the family for Valentine's Day. I watched him as he stood on his tippy toes, watching the machine engrave each tag, with the personalized message he had written for each family member. It was just so cute.

Back in December, I had taken Tanner to the mall, where we went to Build-A-Bear. He decided to make stuffed animals for everyone in the family for Valentine's Day. It was so sad to me, because on that day, in that moment, I knew there was a chance he wouldn't be around to give them out. He picked a bear for each of us, and named them, too. He made personalized voices for each bear and recorded them. Each message said, "I love you." So, for Casey's bear, when you squeeze the arm, it said, in Tanner's sweet voice, "I love you Casey." I knew how touching it was, how special it would be, for everyone to have a bear with his voice expressing his love.

With Valentine's Day finally here, Tanner was so happy to give everyone their stuffed animals and dog tags.

2.15.13

The weekend of dance and getting ready to go to Disneyland. I wanted Tanner to come with us and just hang out in the room. He didn't want to. As he had told me before, he would miss his deliveries and pancakes and bacon.

We got to Disneyland and Casey performed her solo. I cried so hard watching her. It was just too much...all of it. I was an emotional wreck. Tanner called me at 11:30 p.m., and he was so sad. "I love you Mommy. I need you Mommy," he said to me. I told him to come to Disneyland. There was a room waiting for him. He wouldn't come. This went on for a while. He finally fell asleep. I couldn't sleep at all.

2.16.13

Casey had her duet today and production tonight. Casey's duet went well. Her production piece was amazing. They placed first overall, and won double platinum. I was just so happy, that she was able to be part of a winning performance like that. She hung out with friends until 1 a.m. It was so unlike her, and I'm so glad she did.

Michael joined us tonight at Disneyland, but Tanner still wouldn't come. "I'll see you on Sunday, Mommy," he told me.

2.17.13

We were finally home. One successful dance weekend under our belt.

2.18.13

Casey went to the dentist. Dr. L is the best. The summer before he got sick, Tanner had an appointment with her. He was telling her how he was getting taller. Dr. L had him stand against the wall, and she marked his height with a pencil. She said to him, "Next time you come in you can see how much more you grew." That's the kind of amazing doctor she is. Sadly, Tanner never had a chance to go back and check his height.

That day, Dr. L told me her aunt had died of a glioblastoma at the age of forty-two. She told me that after her aunt's surgery and aggressive chemotherapy, she was never the same again. She spent two years like that. This is why we were blessed to have him as him...as Tanner. We haven't lost any of that.

2.21.13

Hospice came this morning to check in. There was really nothing to check on. He was the same. They were amazed at how well he was doing.

Casey's blood came back. All normal. Thank goodness. She was okay on that front, now we just needed the same healthy results on her scans.

The feelings of loneliness and despair and anger just mounted. Why was this happening? Tanner. Casey. My mom. I was bitter. I was tired. I just wanted to laugh again. I just wanted to go out and not have to worry. I wanted to run away. I wanted it the way it was. The way it used to be.

I had no break. I was so down. I was so scared of when the end would happen...I just didn't know if I would be able to handle it all.

2.22.13

I talked to a friend of mine, whom I met through this journey. Another family with the mutant p53 gene. Both of her children had the mutant gene and her young son had already passed away. Her daughter had cancer. We talked honestly. She told me that at her daughter's first MRI, the baseline MRI, they found a brain tumor. This was the MRI Casey was supposed to have in a few days. The one that was supposed to tell me she was okay. But that was not the case for my friend's daughter. There are no words. I was even more scared, if that were even possible.

2.23.13

Today I bought Tanner a cash register at Staples. I had always wanted one, when I was younger. We put real money in it and played store. I tried to teach him how to make change. It was our new entertainment.

Tanner ate like shit today. All junk food. At 11:20 p.m. it hit him. He didn't feel well. He threw up. Cheetos.

He cried, "I don't want to go back to the hospital. I love being at home with you, Mommy." He summed it all up. His head hurt. I cried. I was shaking. This was the beginning of the end, I thought.

We went to bed. I didn't sleep. Not one minute.

2.24.13

The first thing I asked Tanner when he woke up was how he felt. Better. But he admitted his head still hurt a little.

I went out with my dad today, just for a few hours. We went shopping. I needed a dress. A funeral dress. Just writing that makes me sick. Yes, I needed to make sure that I had something to wear at Tanner's funeral. But it made me feel better, knowing I have one less thing to worry about. By the end of the day, I found the perfect funeral dress…ugh.

Later that night, Tanner felt better. He was having a good night. Me? I was an emotional wreck.

Casey was having her brain MRI the next day. We had to be there at 6:30 a.m. She told me she was scared. Not so much for the test, but for the results. I told her it was normal to be scared. Greg told her the same. I couldn't tell her how terrified I was for her. I just reassured her that she was a healthy fourteen-year-old. My baby. Both of my babies. What the fuck.

2.25.13

We woke up and went early for the MRI. Casey first had to get an IV in her arm (for the contrast). The same pediatric unit that sedated Tanner put in her IV. They remembered us. I told them Casey was not like Tanner (Tanner freaked out the last time we were there). She would be fine.

Memories flood back. Five and a half months ago, I was sitting in an MRI room with Tanner. As I rubbed Casey's feet and hand, I recalled last September when this nightmare began. I looked over to the technician to see if I could make out his face through the tinted glass. I wanted to read his expressions. Did he see something? Anything?

The noise of the MRI machine was awful. Even with the earplugs they give you, you can still hear the loud noise of the machine. One of the sounds reminded me of an old phone ringing, the rotary phone at my grandma and grandpa's home, in the years before answering machines, when the phone would ring and ring and ring. Answer it already.

I stared at Casey and filled her with all my love. The MRI helmet she was strapped into had a mirror, and every now and then we made eye contact. I wanted my eyes to tell her eyes that it would be okay. Except I didn't know if it would be okay. But it just had to be.

About forty-five minutes later the MRI ended.

I was exhausted and nervous and anxious all day. They told me it would take two days to get the results. I knew from Dr. T that I would get them sooner.

That afternoon, Dr. T called to say all is okay. Thank you. Thank you. Thank you. I am not sure who I am thanking, but still say the words aloud…Thank You.

The following Monday they would do the other MRI, a whole body scan. I pray for the same healthy results. Please.

I had thought a lot about this mutant gene…the p53. It was never a secret that both Tanner and Greg were carriers. For now, we just kept it quiet that Casey had it. But it got back to me that some people were talking….questioning.

Why would we even consider testing Casey? Why would we do that to her? Which brings up the question...

"*Do* you test your child for something like this?" *Do* you want to know? *Why* would you want to know, if you can't change anything? *What's* the point?

There is a big point.

Seven months before Tanner was diagnosed, we started him on daily shots of growth hormones.

Tanner was short. I'm petite and Greg was a late bloomer, so we weren't too concerned. But then we were told, by his doctors, that they estimated Tanner would grow to about 5'3."

We started seeing an endocrinologist every six months, each time putting off the treatment of growth hormone shots. Finally, about a year ago, when Tanner was ten-years-old, we decided to start the shots, so he could get the greatest benefit out of this treatment. I remember asking the doctor, "Are there any side effects we need to worry about?" The only thing he said was Tanner's hands could possibly get bigger. We could deal with big hands.

When you go to a doctor's office, what's the first thing you do? Fill out forms. And what's always on those forms? Family history. I had always put down, on both Casey's and Tanner's forms, that their paternal grandmother had breast cancer in her early thirties and died at forty-nine. Always. Not once did anyone look at our family history, or even bring up the fact that cancer was in our family. Yes, it was only one cancer, but cancer at a young age is a red flag. And yes, I know just because you have cancer in your family doesn't mean you have a hereditary cancer gene...but what if? *What if you do?*

One thing is for sure...you do not give growth hormones to someone with a hereditary cancer gene. So, if a doctor know this, why wouldn't they bring this up to all patients who are getting hormones? It was not just they could get "big hands," it was so much more than that. Regardless, whether your family history shows cancer or not, a doctor giving a child growth hormones should tell the family that in very rare cases, where someone might carry a hereditary cancer gene, growth hormones should absolutely not be used. Then the information is out there and the family can decide what to do.

I pride myself on being the most proactive parent. I am always on top of everything. I usually am never afraid to speak my mind and tell a doctor or medical professional if I don't think something is right. But I didn't have the knowledge to speak up about this. You do not and would not, give someone with a mutant cancer gene, like p53, hormones. We would never know for sure, if the growth hormones caused the cancer, but I think it might have triggered it.

So now, think about it. Knowledge is power. Yes, it was scary to find out information about having a hereditary cancer gene, but think how different things would have been if we had known. We never would have given Tanner growth hormones. We would have been monitoring him, as we do Casey, and we would have detected anything abnormal right away. He never had a chance, but now that we know this information, Casey does.

March 2013

First day of March. We survived February. Onward.

Tanner went to clinic this morning and completely freaked out. It was a madhouse there. Busier than I had ever seen it. We waited and waited. I just don't get it. I don't understand it. How were there so many sick kids? And with cancer? It is a question that really needs to be looked at, addressed and answered. This was not okay. At all.

Tanner finally got his blood taken, and when the nurse took the needle out, he bled more than usual. I started to get nervous. This could mean a platelet issue. After a while, the bleeding finally subsided, but he was very upset. We finally saw Dr. T, and she said we could go home, just like Tanner wanted.

Later, Dr. T called Greg. Blood counts were fine...no platelet issue. I breathed a sigh of relief. We would start cycle four of Etoposide on Sunday.

3.4.13

Monday.

Casey had her baseline whole body MRI today. Greg took her, while I drove around with Tanner waiting for them to be done. Please let it be okay.

Later that afternoon, we heard from Dr. T that Casey's MRI came out clean. Prayers answered...for now.

3.6.13

Sometimes I just sit and think back to day one. Reflect on everything. Were there signs? Could I have known? I think back to last summer. Tanner seemed more needy. He loved camp, yet he didn't want to go anymore. He wanted to be with me.

Six days before he was diagnosed, we were in Target in the toy aisle. I told him he could pick out a toy. He looked and looked and then turned to me and said, "Mommy something is wrong with my brain. It's too hard to think." I panicked, the way a mom would panic, and texted Greg. Greg didn't respond, and I just dealt with it. I told Tanner he could pick any toy he wanted...and he did...and that was the end of that.

I sometimes think back to that night in Target. What was he telling me? Did he know something was going on? Here was a kid with speech, processing and language issues, and he was able to tell me that something was wrong with his brain. It made no sense...but then it did. Maybe the brain knew...maybe Tanner knew on a totally different level.

3.10.13

Mar 10 day is Marlo day. I have been celebrating this for years. It was because Mar 10 looks like Marlo. Those near and dear know this...and they acknowledge it every year...Mar 10 = Marlo day.

Tonight, Tanner told me something was wrong. It was his head. "It's acting crazy, like wooooo." "Dizzy?" I asked. He couldn't describe it. He cried to me. I told him I loved him so much. He was my hero. He was so good. He told me he's not good. I told him he was, and I will love him the most, always and forever.

3.11.13

I was constantly thinking about what life was like before all of this. When all was good. I missed the good times, with the ones I loved. I missed the ME from back then. I missed being with the people that made me feel like ME. I wanted to escape. To run. To laugh again. I did this often. I thought about my past...before this nightmare began. I so wanted to go back to how it was.

3.12.13

We had to go to clinic today. We were on our way and Tanner said, "Mom, we have to talk. I'm scared." It was such a moment of clarity and maturity. It just blew me away. He was scared. A scared little boy.

3.13.13

I took Tanner to Castle Golf…a miniature golf place. It was a great morning. He was so happy. You could see it in his smile. The old Tanner. I loved days like today.

3.16.13

Tonight was Casey's first night of dance competition at Hall of Fame. It was a local competition in Redondo Beach, so we didn't need to spend the night. Tanner wanted to be with us and watch Casey dance. Casey won two platinum and one high gold with her teams. It was a good night for her.

3.17.13

Casey performed her solo tonight and she was amazing. She won first place platinum and was chosen to perform in Las Vegas at Nationals. I was so glad Tanner was there to watch Casey. It was a moment Casey will carry with her forever. It would be the last time he would see her dance.

3.21.13

I talked to Dr. T. We had another MRI scheduled for the following week. Again, I just didn't see the reason. We were not changing anything.

I just wanted to make Tanner happy. We would go out and do what he wanted to do. He had a life. That's what made him happy. Hospital stays, being neutropenic, going multiple times to clinic... that was not Tanner. He deserved to live each day to its fullest.

3.22.13

Greg has his colonoscopy today. One of the tests he needed to have after finding out he carried the mutant p53 gene. They found fourteen polyps. This was not good. They couldn't remove them all, but they took biopsies. Waiting to hear more.

3.24.13

We went to visit my mom at the hospital...me, Tanner, Casey and Greg.

We drove up to the hospital and Tanner said "Mommy, Daddy, remember when I was here last year?" It broke my heart. We all wore hospital masks and went to visit my mom for a few minutes. It was all very emotional for me. What a journey it had been... these past six months started in the walls of this hospital.

3.25.13

First day of spring break. We all slept in.

I have thought more and more about Greg. He never would have had a colonoscopy had it not been for Tanner and the mutant p53 gene. He would have waited seven more years...until he was fifty years old. There would have been no need to do it sooner. He had no family history of colon cancer. Greg needed to talk to more doctors to see what his options were. He didn't have cancer...yet.

Casey. Greg. Tanner is their angel. Telling them to watch out for their bodies. That they had this fucking mutated cancer gene.

3.26.13

I spoke to Dr. T and cancelled the MRI.

Dr. T said something to me that I couldn't get out of my head. She told me, "You have taught me. I have learned from you." She admitted that in the beginning, it was hard for her to stand back and let me lead the way, when it came to Tanner's treatment. I had called the shots and the shots have been called right.

Each treatment really needs to be individualized. You have to look at the *person* and determine what treatment you do. What are the pros and cons? Quality vs. quantity. Love, laughter, fun, doing what you want to do each and every day was key. And that is what I have done for Tanner.

I didn't need an MRI to tell us the cancer was spreading. We had to just live each day. And that was what we were doing.

3.28.13

It was a clinic day, and I was so anxious. Tanner and I both hated clinic days. Dr. T hadn't seen him for a while, and she didn't see any physical signs of change.

There was a shortage of his oral chemotherapy drug, Etoposide. For the first time, I wondered what if we don't do this anymore? I knew we should. I knew we must. But was this a sign? It was supposed to come in from the manufacturer that week, so we waited to see what would happen.

3.30.13

Tanner woke up with a smile and said, "I love you Mommy." It was what he told me every morning, as soon as he woke up.

The morning went by as usual, but then he told me, "I don't feel well." He said his eyes were tired. His eyes bothered him. He said they were blurry. This continued, and he was uncomfortable and scared and upset. I called hospice. No answer. I emailed Dr. T, and she called me right away. She suggested we go to the emergency room for a CAT scan. We weren't even supposed to do CAT scans, because of the radiation, but in this case, it was quick and would tell us what was going on. It could be the tumor growing or fluid building, which would mean surgery. We really didn't have a choice…a CAT scan was worth doing.

The situation was bad enough that Tanner was okay with going to the emergency room (shit, it must really be bad). "As long as we don't have to stay in the hospital," he said. I promised him we wouldn't. I spoke to the doctor on call, Dr. R. I told him to prepare the emergency room that we were coming in, but just for the scan.

On the way to the hospital, Tanner said to me, "Mommy, I have to get better." My heart just sank.

We got to the emergency room. It was not crowded, but we still had to wait. Tanner was upset and wanted to go home, but he did the CAT scan. Dr. T would call us to review the results, but Dr. R already told us exactly what we didn't want to hear. Even though the scan didn't show as much as the MRI, it showed the tumor had grown. There was no blood or hemorrhaging or fluid, so nothing would need immediate surgery or attention. The tumor was growing and pressing against the brain. Tanner felt the pressure. There was edema…swelling.

We went home, and Tanner was feeling better. I was supposed to meet a friend for dinner, but I cancelled my plans. This was the way it was going to be from now on. I would be home with him…always…until the end.

Dr. T called us. She had not seen the scan personally, but had talked to Dr. R. We discussed putting Tanner on steroids to help with the swelling, which we hoped would help his eyes. I wanted to start him on a low dose.

Our lives were changing. This was another turning point.

3.31.13

It was Easter. One of my best friends, Kim, sent the kids personalized Easter baskets, and Casey and Tanner found all of the eggs I had hidden for them. But it was not a good morning for Tanner. He said to me, "Mommy, something is wrong with the TV. It's broken. It's all blurry." The TV was fine…it was something with his eyes. My dad came over. He saw the difference in Tanner. We just sat there and cried.

I spoke to Dr. T again. We decided to get the steroids and start them today. She told me I needed to speak to hospice. They had to start getting more involved.

April 2013

April Fool's Day.

We started the steroids last night, and Tanner has not complained about a headache or eye issues since yesterday afternoon.

Hospice came by today, and they will start coming once a week. I was drained.

So many people ask about me. How I am. My answer was always the same: this was not about me. But it was...it was about my family...it was about my son...a part of me. All I could say was that I had no choice. I wish I did. So the answer is that I put one foot in front of the other each and every day. I was on autopilot.

I woke up. I cuddled with Tanner. We played "Four Pics, One Word" on my phone. We watched *SpongeBob* and *Caillou* and MGM cartoons and *Diners, Drive-ins and Dives*. We waited for Casey to come home. I cuddled with Casey. I listened to Dave Matthews Band. I Instagramed. I Facebooked. I stopped watching every

TV show except *Homeland* and *Girls.* I read *The Fault in Our Stars* and cried. I shopped online. I made slutty brownies with Casey. I went to the Famers Market every Sunday, and bought fresh roses, because they always brighten up a room and made me smile. I had crumbs in my bed from Tanner's Subway sandwiches, and I didn't care. I redecorated Casey's room, and it looked beautiful. I didn't go out much. I didn't talk on the phone much. I didn't meet my girlfriends for girl's night out like I used to. I was no longer the planner. I was no longer the person I used to be. I would never be again.

As I spent each moment with Tanner, I tried to balance making life as "normal" as it could be for Casey. I was proud of her in so many ways. Her academics. Her dancing. Her maturity. Her having to grow up so fast and making constant adjustments and compromises. As she finished eighth grade and was headed to high school in the fall, I thought back to when I was her age. Certainly not dealing with the issues she is dealing with. It was 1984, and all was good. I remember finishing eighth grade...my Bat Mitzvah...going to TV show tapings...kisses with my boyfriend... going on Teen Tour that summer...taking the bus to the beach and getting ready to start Beverly Hills High School. I wish life could be, would be, so easy for Casey.

And then there was my mom. As I continued to spend each moment with Tanner, I prayed every day for my mom to get better.

Not being by her side and not having her by my side had been very difficult. It certainly was not easy for her to fight her illness, while at the same time not being here helping Tanner fight his. Again, we had no choices.

4.3.13

I spoke to Dr. T today. I told her about Tanner's persistent cough. It could be a cold or allergies...especially since we all had a little something then. Or it could be the excess saliva.

The oral chemotherapy drug finally came in and Tanner started it again last night. Fifth cycle. Dr. T told me he didn't have to come to clinic anymore. Not even for Pentamidine. This warmed my heart. It was the one thing he hated and we didn't have to do that anymore. Although I realized this must mean Dr. T knew that we were nearing the end.

She said it could be weeks, but she had been wrong before. She basically wanted hospice more involved, with his medications and making him happy and comfortable. I asked her one of my dreaded questions: what could we expect as it got toward the end? She told me... seizures, possible secretions (what is a secretion and where will it be coming from?), sleeping a lot...maybe eighteen hours a day. I needed to be prepared for the bad stuff...the really bad stuff.

The steroids were working. He had a good day.

A few months ago, when Dr. T told us Tanner had "weeks to months," I knew I had to start thinking about the terrible and inevitable...Tanner's funeral. The last thing I wanted to do was plan a funeral, but I also knew I didn't want to plan it at the last minute. Everything had to be in order. I didn't know when his death would happen, but I knew all the plans had to be in place.

I am a very Type A person, used to taking control and doing things on my own. My son's funeral? A totally different situation. I needed someone to help me, guide me and plan for me, and it had to be someone I trusted and loved.

I called one of my best friends, Alyson, who owns an event planning company, Levine Fox Events. If anyone could help plan a funeral, it was Alyson. It had to be perfect and Alyson, along with her mom, Diane, would make sure it was. I was thankful to have their help.

It was also a few months ago, after that November day in Dr. T's office, that I told my dad we needed to plan where Tanner would be buried. We knew which cemetery we wanted, but I had one request: there had to be a bench. A bench where I could sit for the many, many times I would be there. I also had this weird issue (well, maybe it was not so weird)...I wanted a plot. A family plot...at least for Tanner and myself. I didn't want him in the ground next to a stranger. It had to be our own private area.

My dad and Grant did the research and showed me what they had found. It was the perfect spot.

4.4.13

The cough seemed to be the only thing that was bothering Tanner.

It was 7:23 p.m. Casey was at dance. Greg was out. It was just Tanner and me. He was napping. Again. He had been tired all day. Our feet were touching. I felt his warmth and wanted to remember it always.

4.5.13

Tanner woke up and his tummy hurt. His cough hurt. He was spitting a lot. "What's wrong with me?" he asked. "Am I going to be okay?" he asked.

4.6.13

He was having a great day. A really good day. As if the other bad days hadn't happened.

We spent time in bed. I held him. He told me: "I love you. You're my sweet girl, Mommy." My heart melts.

4.7.13

You know the Phil Collins song, "I Don't Care Anymore"? That's how I felt about everything. I felt numb. I felt sick. I threw up all the time. I knew something was going to happen…soon. In a horrible, awful way I just wanted things to happen, because it was *going* to happen.

4.8.13

Hospice came over. We talked. They checked his cough. His chest seemed fine.

Dr. T called. We talked. I asked her more about the CAT scan we had done the previous week. The last time we spoke she had not personally seen the report. Now she had. She confirmed it all. The tumor was growing. It was pushing against both sides of the brain. It was growing slowly, but growing. There was nothing more to do.

I told her his tummy hurt. We didn't know, if it was from the steroids or the chemotherapy. She told me that if it was from the chemotherapy, we should stop it. At this point, it was doing nothing. Maybe slowing things down a little, but nothing was helping.

Dr. T asked me if Tanner was asking questions. "Yes. Every five minutes he asked if he was okay," I said. She told me to just continue what we were doing. Make him happy. We were at the point where all treatments would be stopped. We didn't need to come in anymore. No more blood. No more needles. No more poking. We were done. The oral chemotherapy would be the last thing to stop. That's something Greg and I would need to discuss.

I was reading an article about a boy who had brain cancer and was given the chance to play for a Nebraska football team. Tanner saw me looking at the article. There was a picture of the boy, with no hair, in the hospital with his parents. Tanner scrolled to the picture and said, "That boy, he's sick like me." Heartbreaking. Honestly. Simply heartbreaking.

Even though Tanner didn't "look" sick…he still had his head of hair (he never lost it)…he looked at that boy with no hair and knew they were the "same." Yes, Tanner asked me often if he was okay, but he knew the answer…that he wasn't.

I have a headache. Every headache I have had, in these past seven months, has been on the left side. Tanner's tumor was on the left side. I was feeling his pain.

I was on overdrive. I was pissed at everything. At everyone. It was not anyone's fault. It was me. I was just tired of it all. My baby was dying.

I cried so hard tonight. So much. So hard. I couldn't help it. Tanner asked what was wrong. Why was I sad? He answered his own question, "It's because I'm sick?" "Yes," I replied.

4.11.13

I spoke to both hospice and Dr. T. We decided to take Tanner off the oral chemotherapy to see if it helped his tummy. Tonight would be the first night without it. Taking a break wouldn't really make that much of a difference, but we would see if it helped. We would reduce the steroids the next day, as well.

I went out with Gayle tonight. We had drinks, while Casey was at dance. It was nice to be with her.

4.12.13

Second night with no chemotherapy. First day with the reduced dosage of steroids. We would see what happens. At one point he had me put my hand on his head…always the sign of a headache.

4.13.13

Saturday. I had an awful night with him. I noticed his breathing was hard. Fast and hard. I watched him sleep and breathe almost all night long. I even recorded it. It just didn't sound right.

I noticed he was walking heavily on the right side. A sort of limp, one of the things we were told to look out for.

4.14.13

I finally connected with another mom, who had lost a child. I had never met her. We had a few friends in common, and I was told I should talk to her. Her son had died several years before. I could tell instantly that she was someone I could talk to and that I could ask her anything. And so I did. I wanted to know what happens. What happens when it is finally over. When death happens. I was so afraid I was going to bolt. I needed to hear from someone else about this part. Not a doctor. She was honest. She told me what she could.

In the beginning, when Tanner was first diagnosed, all I wanted to do was talk to people who had success with cancer. Who were in remission. Who beat the dreaded GBM (and there weren't many).

Now, it was different. All I wanted to do was talk to moms who had lost their children. I wanted the real, raw details. I wanted to know everything...even the things a doctor might not want to tell you. I needed to hear it all...the honest truth. I think what I needed most was to prepare myself for the worst moment in my life. I didn't have the tools - no one does, until it happens to you.

So I needed to talk to people who had experienced the entire horror...and survived.

Tanner's teachers, Mrs. Washington, Ms. Peters and Ms. Ashley, came over to visit. Tanner was breathing heavily as he visited with them. He interacted with them, but he was tired. You could see it was hard for him.

Michael went with me to visit my mom. It was a difficult visit. She was not doing well...physically, mentally, emotionally. She needed to get stronger. She needed to make this illness empower her. I love my mom and felt so sorry for her. This timing sucked. This disease sucked. I prayed she got through this.

Tanner was getting big and bloated. It was the steroids.

4.15.13

Not an easy night's sleep. He was up a lot. The difficulty of breathing.

Hospice was coming today. They needed to check his breathing...it could be the steroids or the weight gain from the steroids. Or something else.

Today a lunatic planted bombs at the Boston Marathon. Reports say three people died and there were scores of injuries...many amputees. Among the dead was an eight-year-old boy. What the fuck. I grieved for this boy, for his mother. I am about to know her pain. Life changes in an instant. That I already know.

4.17.13

Casey had another dance competition coming up, this time in Irvine, which is about an hour away. I discussed it with Tanner, and he said he was okay with me leaving; he would be with Greg for the weekend.

I planned to window shop at South Coast Plaza on Saturday (anything to keep my mind busy) and then splurge at the Spa at Pelican Hill on Sunday (I doubted even a massage could take the pain away). I needed some "me" time. I just hoped Tanner would be okay while I was gone.

4.18.13

His breathing was heavy tonight. He was very aware of it. It bothered him. I was supposed to leave tomorrow for Casey's dance weekend. How was I supposed to go with his breathing like this?

4.19.13

I decided to call hospice and order oxygen. Just in case. I also ordered him a wheel chair. Another "just in case."

We left for Irvine for Casey's dance competition. It was so strange to be away from home. Tanner was handling it fine. He was happy and knew he would see me on Sunday.

4.20.13

Today Casey was in dance class all day. I worked out and then went to South Coast Plaza. It was not so simple. Yes, I could be away from it all, but I was not really away from it all. Nothing took my mind off reality.

I went back to the hotel and helped Casey get ready for her duet and teen pieces. A long afternoon and night, but we did it. I had dinner with her dance team and the moms. It was nice for her…for both of us.

I was so proud of Casey…as hard as it was to be away from Tanner…I was so happy to spend this time with her.

Tanner called me late at night, crying. He missed me. Needed me. We discussed him coming down. We decided Greg would bring Tanner down in the morning, and we would switch. Greg would be with Casey and I would take Tanner home. I didn't sleep well.

4.21.13

In the morning, I checked in with Greg. Tanner had decided not to come down. He would wait for me to come home. But a few hours later Tanner called and was anxious for me to get home. I loved his call. His little voice. The way he said, "Mommy." The way he said, "I love you." The way he said, "Bye." Everything. I. Love. How could it be that there will be a day, a time, when I won't hear that anymore? Devastating.

I went to Pelican Hill to work out and get a massage. As I worked out, I got emotional. The tears wouldn't stop. I just stood on the treadmill and cried. As much as I had thought I was prepared for this…I was not.

I told Tanner we would be home at 6:00 p.m., but we cut our day short and got home at 4:00 p.m. We rang the doorbell, and he opened the door. He was not expecting to see us that early. "Surprise!" He was so happy. We cuddled and kissed and kissed and cuddled. It was good to be home.

4.22.13

At midnight he had a headache. I gave him two Tylenol. He was restless and didn't feel well. At 3 a.m. the pain was awful. Horrible. He was crying. Clenching his fists. I called hospice. We gave him steroids right away. He had been off of them for almost forty-eight hours. If the steroids didn't help the pain, we would give him morphine. The steroids helped. He fell asleep. Greg came over, and we slept in bed with Tanner. He was no longer in pain.

Tanner woke up happy. The headache was gone. He ate breakfast. Ordered lunch. We waited for hospice to check in on him. He was okay...for now.

He had a good visit with the hospice nurse. I spoke to Dr. T. She wanted to come and visit him here at home.

I asked both of them, the hospice nurse and Dr. T, separately, if he would make it to the summer. They just didn't know. What we did know was that things were happening.

4.23.13

He was tired. He had trouble breathing, and we used the oxygen for the first time. It seemed to help him.

Tanner wanted to make me a surprise. This was his idea. A card for me for Mother's Day. He worked on it and put it in an envelope. He wrote on the front of the envelope: *DO NOT OPEN UNTIL 5-12-13 MARLO.*

With Tanner being so sick, I didn't do much. I sat in bed next to him as he watched his television shows. I played solitaire on my iPhone. I shopped on the Internet. Anything that would calm me. Sometimes I just browsed, window-shopping on the computer. Sometimes I would buy something. And it made me feel a little better.

Mother's Day was coming up, and I found something I wanted. It was a necklace made by one of my favorite jewelry designers, Jennifer Meyer. I ordered it through this great jewelry store in Dallas, Ylang 23. The necklace was a simple gold nameplate that was engraved: "Casey Tanner."

I hoped I would get my necklace in time for Mother's Day. Honestly? I just wanted it in time before anything happened to him.

4.24.13

In the middle of the night, he was in my arms. Breathing deeply. He inhaled. Then nothing. For a moment, my heart skipped a beat. This was it. That moment. I shook him a little to rouse him, and he breathed again. It was an apnea moment. It was so scary.

Remember that scene in the beginning of *Terms of Endearment*, when Shirley MacLaine goes into the bedroom and pinches her baby to make sure she's alive? Yes, I have been that parent. So many of us have. This moment reminded me of that…I just needed that next breath.

I told Greg about it later, and he told me that one day it would happen. I know it will. But, he said, how peaceful it would have been if that was the way it did happen.

4.25.13

Tanner woke up and was tired. Very tired. His breathing was heavy as well. He came downstairs and fell back asleep again, sitting up on the couch. I knew this was not "him."

I made him pancakes and put the plate next to him. He didn't touch them. I sat down next to him, and he told me he had a headache. I called hospice. I gave him an extra dose of the steroid. In twenty minutes he pepped up. "My headache is gone!" He started eating. He rallied. He's Mr. Rally.

It was a hard day in general. Naps. Oxygen. Both several times. The hospice nurse stopped by for a visit.

Casey had a talent show at school. I didn't go. I didn't feel comfortable going. I felt bad...missing her performance...but I just couldn't do it. It had been a tough day.

4.26.13

He was constantly asking, "Am I okay"? Sometimes I changed the subject. Sometimes I answered him back, "Are you okay?" Sometimes I said, "No. You are sick. There's a boo boo in your brain."

As I have mentioned, Tanner was this *different* kind of kid with speech, language, processing, and communication issues. So it wasn't so cut and dry to simply say, "Tanner you are dying from terminal brain cancer." That just wasn't right for him. The concept of "a boo boo in your brain" was easier.

Honestly, he knew what was going on. He lived the way he lived, he laughed the way he laughed, he played the way he played, because the idea of death wasn't on his mind constantly.

4.28.13

Dr. T came over to visit today. She was pregnant...expecting a girl in October. Tanner slept for most of the visit. She rubbed his head as he slept.

4.30.13

Tomorrow is the first day of May. Eight months since our journey began. The month the kids celebrated their half birthdays. May was a month I always liked.

I put Tanner in the wheelchair and we went into town. It was a good workout for me. We both had to pee, when we got home. Pee too. P2. Like a floor in an office building...we always used to press P2 and laugh. That was our inside joke.

Later on, Casey came home and hung out in bed with us. The three of us. Laughing, playing. It was a moment of normalcy. I took it all in.

May 2013

I got a delivery today. Mama's turn for a delivery. The name plate necklace that I ordered had arrived, and I loved it. It meant the world to me. I reminded myself to send the store a thank you email, for getting it to me "in time."

My mom came over for a little while. She was feeling well enough for a visit, and it was nice. I was glad she was here.

5.4.13

May The Fourth Be With You.

I felt like shit. I finally got sick. Tanner went with me to my ENT. I had a sinus infection.

I was exhausted and just wanted to rest. I started antibiotics and hoped to feel better soon.

5.8.13

Tanner wanted IHOP in the morning. We went, but one bite into the pancakes, he was ready to go home.

On the way back, Tanner asked me, "Am I going to be okay with the boo boo in my brain?" I paused and then answered him, "It's bad…it's not good." He replied, "Yeah, I know." I told him I wished I could make it better, I wished Mommy could change things and make it better, but I couldn't. All I could do was make him happy every day. I started to cry, and he asked what was wrong, but he answered his own question, "It's because I'm sick."

I went out to dinner with Gayle, and while I was gone, Tanner pulled out his loose tooth. A moment of "normal." A moment when he was still just an eleven-year-old kid. He told Greg he pulled it out, because he "needed the money." OMG…brilliant. That was my boy.

5.9.13

I didn't sleep much. I had a dream the hamsters died.

Almost every Sunday, I go to the Farmers Market to get flowers. I love fresh flowers, but there are a few I don't care for, including calla lilies…the white flower with a yellow stem in the middle. I just don't like them. They spook me. I always thought of them as the "death flower." They just remind me of death.

This morning I took our dog, Daisy, out to the front yard. Next to my car, sprouting from the bushes is one flower...a fucking calla lily. I hadn't even known that plant grew in my yard. One flower. Full bloom. Never, in all of the years I have lived in my home, had I seen a calla lily. I had a bad feeling that week...this didn't do anything to help me.

Greg had made the decision to remove his colon, as a preventative measure. Thanks to his having had the colonoscopy when he did, they caught cancer before it became cancer. He consulted with several doctors and, because he carried the mutant gene, everyone said that cancer would most likely occur. Removing his colon would protect him.

Greg was having colon surgery the following Saturday. It was scary. I was scared for him. For us. I hoped everything would be okay. No complications. I hoped his recovery would be okay. Just get it done, make sure there is no cancer and get on the road to recovery.

Tanner didn't look good to me. He was huge. It was the steroids. But something in his eyes...the sparkle...was gone.

5.10.13

Eight months. Eight months since this nightmare began. Tanner was not in a good mood this morning. Confused. Not sure what he wanted to do.

We had a new hospice nurse. He was a nice guy. After he was done checking Tanner, I walked him out and told him everything that had been going on in our lives. It was then that I realized that hearing our story was just…a lot. Tanner getting sick, the chemotherapy not working, being terminal, my mom getting sick, p53 (which most people don't even know about), keeping Casey healthy, Greg and his colon surgery…it was a lot.

5.12.13

I decided to post on Facebook…

It was Mother's Day. Eight months into this journey and today is Mother's Day. Today means a whole lot more than it has ever meant to me. Honestly, I never have felt as if I needed a special day to be celebrated as a Mother, because truly, every day is Mother's Day. Every day I am a Mother. Every day I love and am given love by my two beautiful kids. Every day, in my heart and soul, is Mother's Day. But this Mother's Day will be remembered and cherished and loved. I will relish every moment, bottle it and keep it in my heart forever.

Rainbow Around The Son

I will always appreciate the days leading up to this day. Tanner's excitement while making my card, weeks ago, and putting it in an envelope, telling me I cannot open it until 5-12-13. My kids telling me not to look at the computer, as they went online to order flowers for me on 1-800-Flowers, and then asking me for my credit card number so they can pay for it. My dad taking Casey out to get me a Mother's Day surprise at my favorite store. Tanner and Casey whispering to each other about today, and Tanner looking at me and saying, "Shhh...it's a secret for Mother's Day."

Today I will spend Mother's Day with my beautiful kids Casey and Tanner, with my incredible, funny, brave, awesome best friend of an ex-husband, Greg, and my unwavering, dedicated, loving, strength of a rock boyfriend, Michael. My family. It doesn't matter what we do, but we will spend it together celebrating (can I even say that word?) Mother's Day.

So, where are we? What is going on? All I can say is this. No one, not us, not the doctors, not anyone who knows our situation thought we would be where we are today. Eight months later and Tanner is still making us laugh and smile. My cuddle bug...he is so strong, so brave, so unlike any other kid, person, human being I have ever met. As I have always said, it's all about the moments, good and bad. We don't have answers. We don't know what to expect. We don't know the when's and the what's and the why's.

So scary. So all we can do is take it moment by moment and know the clock is ticking...a little louder than before.

Several years ago, a close friend of mine shared this quote with me, and I find myself reading it aloud daily:

"One day at a time - this is enough. Do not look back and grieve over the past, for it is gone; and do not be troubled about the future, for it has not yet come. Live in the present, and make it so beautiful it will be worth remembering."

Remember that card Tanner made me last month? I finally got to open it, and it said: *Dear Mommy, Happy Mother's Day. We love to cuddle and I like to eat Chin Chin and Marty's burgers and that's it. I hope we can cuddle in bed. I love you. Love, Tanner.*

After a long day, Tanner wanted his Mother's Day cuddles. And, of course, he got them.

Today was a Mother's Day I will always cherish.

5.13.13

My mom came over this morning, and we spent the day after Mother's Day together.

Hospice also came over; Tanner had high blood pressure which is normal with steroids. We might have to medicate him. Another thing to deal with. Ugh.

5.14.13

Tanner woke up late, but he was still tired. He went downstairs, and I made him his peanut butter and jelly sandwich. He fell asleep at the table. He woke up with a headache, and I gave him half a dose of morphine. Forty minutes later he was still in pain. I gave him the other half. He slept. I cried. I told him "I love you" one hundred times in a row. I kept my hand on his head. He told me his head still hurt. Finally, he sat up and said he felt better.

Later, Dr. T called. She said if Tanner's headaches continued for the next few days, Greg should cancel his surgery for Saturday. She also reminded us how Tanner fights this and fights it hard. I sometimes think these headaches are the start of the end. But then Tanner always rallies back.

Tonight we laid in bed with Tanner...holding him. He was falling asleep again, and he was out of it. Greg was on one side and Casey on the other side of me. We were holding him. Loving him. We were all crying. We were telling him how much we loved him. How brave he was. He told us, through closed eyes, "We are a family." He told us, he loved us. He thanked us. We all thought, truly thought, this was it. That this was the moment. And if it was, it would have been okay. It was just the four of us. And then, in true Tanner fashion, he woke up, sat up and asked for the television remote. The moment was over.

My dad called it "The Long Goodbye."

5.15.13

He's back to himself. Tired, but no naps. No headaches. No nothing. Like I said, this kid rallies.

Tanner said to me, "You're the best Mommy and my sweet woman." I melt.

My dad came over today. So did Gayle. I had told her, if she was going to come visit, it should be sooner than later.

My friend Claudio, whom I have known since eighth grade, texted me. He would be in town that weekend cleaning out his dad's office. Back in December, his dad had been ill. We had made plans to have dinner, and on that day, the day we were to meet, his dad passed away. I just can't believe that was five months ago.

Claudio asked if he could come and visit us, and I was okay with that. To be honest it was something I was looking forward to. I had allowed very few friends over, and he was one of those friends that I just knew would bring smiles to our faces. We made a plan for Saturday.

5.16.13

Another morning. Another headache. Maybe this was the pattern? We increased the steroids to ten milligrams and gave him morphine. Two hours later he was okay, and the headache was gone. He hardly napped during the day, but he looked tired.

I decided to have him make a Father's Day card for Greg. He could hardly write. The letters were confusing to him. I noticed the same thing with his typing on the computer. He had trouble spelling. He asked me, "Mommy, what's wrong with me?"

I am so very sad. I touched him. I looked at him. I breathe him in. So very sad, that it will come to an end sooner than later. I know everyone dies. No one lives forever. But this is just too soon.

5.17.13 - 5.18.13

Headache again this morning. We do the usual...steroids and morphine. He hardly sleeps. He just lay in my lap and talked to me the whole time. Played with my phone and talked to me. About two hours later he got up, and his headache was gone.

I took him early to pick up lunch at Marty's Hamburger Stand. He was so tired. As we waited for our food, I went to the gas station next door. He didn't even pump the gas...something he loved to help me with. He asked me to get the receipt, because he tells me, "I love receipts." He kept nodding off, and I talked to him to keep him awake. Not sure if this was still the morphine or if it was the tumor making him tired.

He dozed off on the way home. We talked at the red light. He said to me, "We are best friends. We kiss. We cuddle. We sleep in bed together." Sigh...I love his words.

Hospice came over. He weighed 111 pounds. His blood pressure was normal.

Tanner told me I was his sweet woman. His cute sweet woman. Greg was at the house all day. He was doing his 'colon prep' for his surgery tomorrow. He would be sleeping over.

Harry, Greg's Dad, who came in town for his surgery, would take Greg to the hospital early in the morning. Renee, his stepmom, would help me with Casey and Tanner for the few days Greg would be in the hospital.

After dinner, Tanner got tired and went upstairs. He was falling asleep a lot. I settled into bed with him, and Casey joined us, and I helped her finish her school project.

Around 11 p.m., Greg took me aside. We closed the door to Casey's room and spoke privately and truthfully. He asked me what he should do about his surgery. I told him to do it. Tanner would be okay. I would take care of him. But, I said, if something is meant to be, and if something was going to happen to Tanner, it would happen in the middle of the night. Never in a million years would I think this would ring true.

At 2:40 a.m. Tanner woke up. Horrible headache. I get Greg. I give Tanner morphine and steroids. It was bad. I got a cold washcloth and kept it on his head.

I talked to him, and talked to him. He told me, "Stop talking Mommy." His head really hurt. He slept and made noises. He threw up. He talked incoherently. I knew something was different.

(I think, sometimes, the mind does things to protect you. This was a moment my mind was protecting me from. Later, after time had passed, Greg reminded me that when Tanner threw up, he said, "I didn't do anything." When Greg said this, I thought he was crazy. "Tanner never said that," I told Greg. "Yes he did," Greg responded. I digested it for a minute and just started to cry and cry. It was coming back to me. He did say it. This destroyed me. Truly destroyed me. I had forgotten and for a very good reason… it was just too sad to remember. He was so brave. But in that moment, with those words, he was a scared, innocent, little boy. I will never get over that memory. It was too powerful. Too devastating. It's a memory I don't like to think about.)

He was sleeping, but breathing very heavily. I called Michael and my dad. I woke Casey. We called hospice. I called my mom and Stan, Grant and my nephew, Jackson. Greg called his parents, Harry and Renee.

By 7 a.m., everyone was here. Tanner was asleep in my bed. We moved him from what was always "his side" to "my side." We surrounded him. We told him we loved him. We held him. We kissed him. We touched him.

We sat this way for hours. At about 10:45 a.m., I looked down at his hands, and I saw his fingernails turning blue. I told everyone Tanner was about to die. We watched him take his last breaths. I didn't know exactly what time he died, but I remember looking at the clock, which read 10:51 a.m. My baby was gone.

Sometimes I wonder if he planned his death. Does that seem weird to say? Let me rephrase that. I think it was orchestrated perfectly. It was a scene that could have been in a movie. Tanner died at home. In my bed. Peacefully. Without that "really bad stuff" happening to him. With our entire family holding him… surrounding him. Greg's parents, who don't even live in California, were there. My mom, who was about to go back into the hospital for her final month-long chemotherapy treatment, was there. Greg, who normally doesn't sleep at my house, was there for every second of that night. Casey, who was supposed to take a high school placement test and had dance tryouts that morning, was there. We were all there…as a family.

I was so proud of myself. The thing I was most afraid of happening…didn't. I thought I would run. I thought I couldn't be there in those final moments. I thought I wasn't strong enough... that I didn't have it in me. You never realize how strong you are, until you are tested. Until the moment presents itself, and then you are in it...100%.

I held onto him until the end, and I stayed with his body for a long time afterwards. The thing I was most afraid about...that I had the most fear about...I had dealt with. As a Mom would. As a Mom should. I brought him into this world...I helped him out of this world. I was there...every step of the way. And for that I was so proud.

5.18.13

A little before noon.

Tanner just died.

My baby will always be in my heart...your sweet woman will always love you.

RIP my baby boy.

For Tanner's entire life, he was in my arms. By my side. Cuddling with his Mama. During the several hours before he passed away, as the family gathered at his bedside, we took our positions. Greg was on one side of him, and I gave up my permanent spot of holding him in my arms. I gave that to Casey. I don't know why or how or what made me do that. I just did. I was on his left side next to his feet. My body faced his body. I intertwined my legs with his, just as we had slept for many a night, and I held onto his webbed toe, that I loved so. I did not let go…at all.

I texted those closest to me, and told them that Tanner was gone. My best and dearest friends…they needed to hear it directly from me, before it became "social media public." I texted Alyson who, with her mom, needed to start coordinating the funeral and luncheon.

After about two hours, we knew it was time for the mortuary to pick him up. I didn't want to be present for this. Not at all. I let go of his toes, I unwrapped my legs from his, and I knelt down to kiss my baby a sweet, final goodbye.

We all went into Casey's room. Into her bed. All of us. Greg and Michael stayed behind in my room with Tanner, to be there when the mortuary workers arrived

I heard strange steps outside Casey's door. I knew they were there to take him. I had Casey put on her music…loud. I didn't want to hear a thing.

Now what? What did we do now? We didn't know what was right or what the rules were. Are there rules? I don't think there are. We would do what felt best for us…for our family.

Casey was priority and what she wanted was most important. So we asked her...what did she want to do? She asked if we could have people over. And so we did. In and out all day and night long. A house full of friends. Full of love. Full of support. Full of food. Full of hugs and kisses. Full of laughter. It was necessary. It was lifesaving.

At some point that day, I went outside to look at the calla lily in my front yard. The one that I had never seen before. The one that sprouted earlier this week. The one that I had a bad feeling about. I took a pair of scissors and cut it. I didn't want it to grow... not anymore.

5.19.13

The day after. I woke up at 5 a.m. and watched Casey's room fill with light. I slept in her room last night. The first sunrise without my baby.

This feeling of loss is unreal. No words. I felt as if I were missing something. It was too quiet. I kept thinking I needed to check on him.

I called my dad on his home phone. When I dialed, there was a sort of electric static. It was not like the bad reception you get on a cell phone. It was electricity. I was confused and hung up. But then I got it...isn't it things like electricity and lights that you hear about when the departed are trying to contact us? To reach us? I was aware that I needed to start looking for signs. Everywhere. Anywhere. I thought, maybe that was Tanner.

We went to the cemetery. I asked to meet the person who was looking over Tanner's body. Her name was Michelle. She was a mom, too. I hugged her. I asked her to whisper in Tanner's ear and tell him how much I love him.

When we came back home, I was a mess. People were coming over, and I just couldn't deal. It was too hard, but what choice did I have? So, I took a deep breath and dealt with it. I had to...for Casey...for Tanner.

Later on, I completely lost it. I sat with my mom, dad and Grant...at the top of my staircase...and we talked. We talked about what happened right after Tanner died. I needed a day to process it. We all did. I didn't write about it yesterday, but I was ready to digest it all now.

Right after Tanner took his last breath, the most incredible thing happened...to me.

I had seen that Tanner's fingernails had turned blue. A friend had told me about this. Something that often happens right before someone passes away. I had been constantly checking them the night before and through the night. When I saw that his nails were blue, I told everyone it was about to happen. He was going to die. I didn't know why or what or how. I had never been with someone who was dying. I had never experienced this, yet I knew. I was so in sync with him that I knew.

We watched him take his final breaths. In and out. In and out. And then they stopped. He had died. I suddenly felt this heaviness, this feeling, this warmth, this thing. I couldn't label it...there were no words to describe it. It was in my heart. In my chest. Something I had never felt before. Something I don't think I will ever feel again.

Everyone was crying but me. I started to speak in a loud, unfamiliar voice: *"We love you Tanner. You saved your dad. You saved your sister. Today is the first day of a new beginning. We will honor you, Tanner. You are our hero."*

And then I was quiet; that strange feeling rushed out of me. It went away as fast as it had come, and then I started to cry. I collapsed in tears. It was him. He was talking through me. His soul stepped into mine, said the words he needed to say and then went to heaven. That's what I believe. Recalling what had happened with my mom, dad and Grant brought it all back. They agreed with me. There was no doubt about it...Tanner's soul was in mine.

Even now, as I sit back and think about that moment...it was surreal. I mean, who does that? What mom, who has just lost her child, speaks in a voice that is unfamiliar and preaches, as if she were giving a sermon? There was no explanation. It just made no sense. Except that it was him. It was Tanner's soul in mine. It was Tanner's words through my mouth. It was Tanner's message to us all.

Later that night, Greg, Casey and I sat in the living room. Each of us had our laptop computer. We were quiet. All you could hear were the tap-taps of the keyboard. The three of us sat there and wrote our eulogies for Tanner's funeral.

There was never any debate. We knew we would all speak. It was what was supposed to be. In the end, Greg suggested having Michael say a few words as well. I'm glad he did. Michael had developed such a close relationship with Tanner…it was appropriate.

As we planned his funeral, we realized how Tanner's loss was truly felt by so many. It wasn't just us, the immediate family that was mourning; so many others were mourning too. We knew this would not be a small funeral. People from our whole lives, from Tanner's whole life, would be there. Tanner made an impact on so many. We always knew this, but after his death we realized it so much more. Those who knew him. Those who didn't. So much love for my boy.

Rainbow Around The Son

5.21.13

Today was my son's funeral.

We arrived at the cemetery and, instead of sitting in a room behind a curtain, we stood outside and greeted our guests. I think people were surprised at this, but this is who we are. I had never seen so many people at a funeral. I was later told there were over 500 in attendance.

I had left the planning and details - everything - in Alyson's and Diane's hands, and as funerals go, this one was pretty amazing. Every touch, every moment was exactly as it should be. From the program to the life-size SpongeBob decorated in flowers...yes, it was exactly as it should be.

Before Tanner died, I would sometimes imagine myself at his funeral. Crazy, I know, but I knew it was inevitable. So, sometimes late at night, when I couldn't sleep, I thought: How would I feel? What I would wear? Who would be there? Would I be able to get through it? I allowed myself to think all of these thoughts.

I have never been nervous speaking in front of an audience, but this was different. It wasn't about nerves...it was about composure. This was my son's funeral, and I had to be as poised as I could be, as I spoke about Tanner.

I knew what would help...I needed to make sure there would be a special someone out there, in the hundreds of people who were in attendance, who would keep me calm. Yes, my family would be there...all in the front row. Yes, my best friends would be there...scattered all around. But I needed one person, my go-to person, whom I trusted, loved and felt safe with. So that, if at any moment I faltered, I could look into their eyes and know I would be okay. I asked a very close friend of mine to be my life line. And so he was.

I looked at the sea of faces...friends sitting before me, friends standing outside, since the crowd was so big. I knew friends in other parts of the country were watching via live stream. I scanned the crowd and found my person. Our eyes met, I took a deep breath, and the words just came spilling out:

Many people here "knew" Tanner. You knew my sweet guy. But many of you just knew him from the past eight months...because you followed this journey. You have gotten to know him from my Facebook posts, from Greg's, from Casey's. But there's so much more, so much. So, let me tell you a little about Tanner. The funniest, most cuddly, loveable kid I know.

The day Tanner was born, the doctor handed him to me, and I did the "mom thing to do." I counted his fingers and toes. Five fingers, check. Another five fingers, check. Five toes, wait... Yes, there were five toes, but he had a webbed toe. Does that count? It's still five toes...it just was different, but it counts. I loved holding those toes. My guy with the funny toes. I never would have thought it was those web toes that I would hold onto until the end...as he took his last breath, and hours after. And I did. And I didn't let go of those toes.

Tanner was the best baby ever. So good. He ate, he slept...and in his own crib. Unlike Casey who had to sleep every night in our bed, Tanner liked his room, his crib, his space (of course that changed years later, when he would only sleep in my bed and never in his own). After Tanner was born, one of my dad's dear friends said to my dad: "Tanner Jay Longstreet. That's the name of someone who is going to go places. Everyone should know Tanner." How right he was.

When Tanner was two and a half, he had reached every milestone, except he didn't talk. We figured it was nothing. He was a boy, a younger sibling, and he had a sister that never stopped talking. We took him to a speech therapist, and we never knew that was just the beginning of a very long road of therapy, doctors and services. No one could define him. There was no "label" for him. He was challenging. He was stubborn. He was strong willed. And he was the greatest kid ever. Like his web toe being different, Tanner was different. He didn't have special needs. He was just...special. He wasn't the typical kid. I know that scared some people and yes, some people just didn't get him, but the ones who made the effort, the ones who really saw him, they saw a kid who was just, amazing. Simply amazing.

Marlo Gottfurcht Longstreet

This picture on the program sums him up. It's an old picture, but one that puts a smile on our face every time we look at it. We were at Disneyland. He was maybe five years old. We were in line for Dumbo and, unbeknownst to me, he had to go to the bathroom. He didn't want to lose his place in line, and we were almost at the front. It was then that I realized he didn't wait to make it to the bathroom, and he went in his pants. I had to change him, but I had nothing to change him into. He had a long sleeve shirt and so I slipped it on over his waist. I tied the sleeves in front. It looked like a skirt. He thought it was hysterical. And he was wearing nothing underneath. That is that picture...he's doing his little Tanner dance with his "skirt." Of course, to make it a typical Tanner story, as we were heading past the castle, a Disneyland employee asked if we wanted a family picture. We said yes. We said cheese, and as we did Tanner lifted his "skirt" up and showed everyone the goods. That was true Tanner. A comedian. Perfect comedic timing. That was Tanner.

In kindergarten at Marquez, while the other kids were playing games, Tanner was making an Amazon wish list on the class computer. In first grade, he had to wait outside of the classroom and make sure everyone was there every day. He would know who didn't come, and if someone was absent, he just didn't want to stay at school. He wanted his class to be complete. In second grade, he broke his arm and loved coming back to school in his cool blue cast. In third grade, all the kids had to do this math program online and complete each level. Tanner was really good at math and loved this program. He figured out all of his fellow student's passwords and would go onto their accounts and complete their levels for them. That was Tanner.

Last year, for fourth grade, he started Village Glen School. He loved his teacher and would help her go online to tell her what DVDs to check out from her local library to bring to class each week. At Village Glen, students take taxicabs to school. He was in Taxi 6321. Tanner had such a fascination with the taxis that anywhere in town, if we saw a taxi (it had to be a minivan yellow taxi), we would call out the taxi number, and he would be able to tell us if it was a "school taxi." Many times we would text him a taxi number from the road, and he would answer "No" if it wasn't a school taxi and "Yes" if it was. That was Tanner.

Last summer, Tanner told me about this DVD series he watched at school: "Holidays for Kids." He wanted to get the DVDs. I, of course, said yes, until I went online and saw how much they cost (the complete series was over $800). I told him "no way." About a week later, Casey and I were home, and the doorbell rang. It was UPS. With a big box. Addressed to Tanner. I open it up. It was the DVDs. With an invoice for over $1,000 (with tax and shipping). Tanner had taken my credit card (I knew nothing about this) and ordered the DVD's. When I was looking at the invoice to see what he did, I noticed they asked him what Institution he was with. He wrote in... Popeye University. That was Tanner.

The first day of school this year, the first day of fifth grade, his taxi driver was late getting him home...lots of traffic and she took a different way. The next day I get an email from Amazon confirming my order. Tanner had ordered his driver a GPS system for her to put in her taxi...so she could get him home faster and never get lost. That was Tanner.

Tanner truly marched to his own drum. He was stubborn. He was tough. But at the same time, he was the sweetest, kindest, most empathetic, funny, cuddly kid. Charming, loveable, memorable...this is what I called his saving grace. He could be a pain in the ass one minute, making his own rules, not listening to anyone, and the next minute he's winning Student of the Year awards at his school. He was the funniest kid. He knew what was funny, and when it was funny. He said funny things. He knew how to make people laugh... adults and kids alike. That's what many will remember. How he made them laugh. And he laughed. A hearty laugh. He had a laugh that was infectious. Late at night, he would watch MGM cartoons, and he loved this one cartoon, Droopy. Sometimes it would be so late, I would fall asleep, and he would still be up watching. I would wake up to him laughing so hard at those cartoons he found funny. While he loved his "kid" shows, he also loved adult humor. He loved, Robot Chicken. He loved, Jackass. He loved the movie Airplane. Things that were inappropriate. His ring tone when he called me was the song SexyBack. That was Tanner.

He loved elevators. If you were going to a hotel or to an office building, he would ask you to take a picture of the elevator. He was able to tell you if the elevator was an Otis, a Thyssenkrupp, a Kone or Schindler. He would watch YouTube videos of this guy, Diesel Ducy, who posted videos on elevators. Tanner had seen every one. That was Tanner.

Tanner loved his videos and electronics. He had this ability to have the TV on, the iPad on, the computer on, and still monitor everything that was going on around him. He would hear your conversations and be aware of everything, even if you think he wasn't. That was Tanner.

He loved his shows: SpongeBob, Caillou, Blues Clues, Little Bill. After he got sick, Tanner started ordering DVD and VHS tapes of his favorite shows from Amazon and eBay. When he ran out of DVDs and videos to watch from the US, he started to buy videos from the UK, Australia and Canada. I had to search for a PAL player that would play videos from other countries. He kept inventory. We must have hundreds of videos at home, yet he never ordered duplicates (unless one was broken or dirty). He knew everything he had. He was so into the UK that it became a joke in the family. Instead of asking if someone was okay, we would say "UK?" And to make Tanner laugh, we would answer with his other favorite country, Australia. "UK?" "Australia." That was Tanner.

One of his favorite rituals throughout his illness was waiting for his deliveries...UPS, Fed Ex, On Trac and USPS. Our whole day revolved around waiting for his deliveries. By the way, that's why he hated Sundays. No mail. He would say, "Nothing to do, nothing to do." We would go outside at 11 a.m. and he would stand in the middle of the street and look down the block. Was the mail truck one block away? Two blocks away? Three blocks away? He would track his deliveries. He would go online to track them, so he knew where they were. In transit. Out for delivery. He knew how many deliveries he was getting each day. If there were a lot, they would be in a USPS plastic bin. We would open them, and if they were new, he would say "plastic" because they were wrapped in plastic. If they were used he would say "not plastic," and I would wipe them down with a wet wipe. He loved his mail. That was Tanner.

Tanner would check the weather every day. He hated rain. He hated thunder. He would wait until midnight to look at the weather thirty days in advance. He only wanted sunny days. The day he left us was a beautiful day. When the sun would shine, he would say, "It's a beautiful day Mommy." That was Tanner.

He was the most loving child. He taught us about love...kisses, hugs, cuddles...the most affectionate kid. Every day, every hour, he *wanted me to cuddle with him. He just wanted me next to him. I would always say to him, daily in fact, "Who loves you the most in the world?" The reply was always the same, "Mommy." He knew how much I loved him. He not only was loved more than anyone I know, he gave more love than anyone I know. That was Tanner.*

People would ask me, if Tanner knew what was going on. Because Tanner wasn't the typical eleven-year-old, it was a unique situation of what he knew and didn't know. On the surface, he was happy-go-lucky every day. Mind over matter. This is why, I believe, he lived as long as he did. But deep down inside, on a level many of us may not understand or comprehend, he knew. One night, late at night, he started to cry and he said to me, "Mommy, I'm dying. My heart is broken. I'm dying." The next morning he had no recollection of this. He knew on a deep, spiritual level. He knew. My magical boy. That was Tanner.

The past eight months have been on borrowed time. The choices we made were based on the person he was. It was quality over quantity. We made every single day happy, fun, filled with love and laughter. We cuddled, we kissed, we had our routines. Whether it was ordering from LA Bites he loved his Lo Mein from Chin Chin (plain with no yuckies) or going to Marty's (three burgers, three fries) or pizza or pancakes or baking brownies. We had our routines. That was Tanner.

Marlo Gottfurcht Longstreet

He expressed his love more than anyone I know. He told me he loved me. He told his father he loved him. His sister, Casey, he told her over and over that he loved her. My dad...he loved my dad. They had this thing. My dad would walk into the room and Tanner would say, "I love you Papa. I'm gonna cry" and my dad would say back, "I love you Tanner. I'm gonna cry." He loved my boyfriend Michael. In fact, he told Michael he loved him just weeks after I met him. We were just friends then...way long before I even knew I loved the guy. Tanner just knew. Tanner loved my mom. She made him his favorite peanut butter and jelly sandwiches, and he loved to play with her and Papa Stan. He loved his uncle Grant, his cousin Jackson and Jackson's car. He loved his Grammie Renee and Grampie Harry (although he didn't love going to Seattle because it was rainy there). He loved his Auntie Stacy in New Zealand (who was always able to get him the Australian DVD's that weren't "worldwide" and couldn't get shipped here). He loved everyone who was in his life. Everyone who touched his life. That was Tanner.

Recently, he turned to me and said, "You're a good woman." Before I could say a word, he continued, "You're my sweet woman. That means I love you." Every day after that he called me his sweet woman. Three days before he passed away (and I know this because I was constantly taking notes, pictures and videos of everything with him), he said to me, "You're the best Mommy and my sweet woman." Who could ask for more? That was Tanner.

Rainbow Around The Son

Throughout his illness, I spent every moment with Tanner. 24/7. I knew his every breath. His every step. I was his voice. His advocate. His best friend. His Mommy. I was his everything, and he was mine. We had this connection that ran deeper than any words can ever describe. It was more than just the "umbilical cord" not being cut thing...it was this connection that only comes once in a lifetime... if even that. He was my guy. My mushy guy. My sweet boy. I miss him terribly. It's so quiet. We keep the TV's on...it's always been the background noise in our house. We keep them on for him. I have no regrets. We did everything right. We said I love you more times than we could count. We kissed and cuddled and laughed. I made every single minute count so there would be no regrets. I'm having withdrawals from his warmth and touch. From his voice and being. I just miss him....my sweet baby boy.

I am a Mom of two kids. I will always be. That is who I am. Mother to Casey and Tanner. I am now a Mom who has lost a child. I am a Mom who will never be complete again. I never wanted to be "that" person. You know what I mean...the person you will now look at differently. The person you look at and just say, "Oh My God... she lost a child." I never wanted to be that person. But if being that person means I was Tanner's Mom, then, as much as it sucks, I'm proud to be that person.

I want to thank everyone. All of us thank you for your love, support, prayers. The past few days have been...wow...no words can describe how they have been. It's the power of social media that has been overwhelming. Every time I went on Facebook, every single time, I saw people dedicate their statuses to Tanner. There are just no words to describe it. Friends from far and near. Tanner's friends. His teachers. His counselors. My friends. People who have never met Tanner. People who have never met me. Tanner has touched us all.

Tanner had a higher purpose. Looking back now, I feel like every moment with him, his differences, his specialness, his strengths and weaknesses, all were there to lead up to this moment. It is now my purpose. My goal. My everything...it's to keep his memory alive. To have his legacy live on. I will do it. You will do it. We all will do it. Keep Tanner alive in our hearts.

In months to come, we will be setting up a Foundation in Tanner's name. You will learn more about it in time, but it is now my purpose. This is what I will be doing...anything to prevent other families from going through what we went through. No one should be dealt with the deck of cards we have been dealt with so it is now my mission, my life, my being, to take this experience and turn it around.

Tanner is our hero. Because of him, others will live. Because of him, others will have a chance. Because of him, our world will be a different place, a better place. He is our hero. My hero.

Rainbow Around The Son

Tanner has changed my life. He has made an impact on your life. If this experience makes you a better person, a better parent, then Tanner has done his job.

If it allows you to let go of the bullshit (Tanner would just have said: "Mommy, no bad words"), then Tanner has done his job.

If it makes you stop and smell the flowers for just a little longer.

To look up at the sky and have the sun shine on your face.

To appreciate the small things and let go of the bad.

To be the bigger person.

To learn to say you're sorry.

To not sweat the small stuff, then Tanner has done his job.

To smile for no reason.

To laugh out loud.

To kiss the person you love.

To tell someone you love them.

To share your feelings.

To not be afraid.

To jump high.

Marlo Gottfurcht Longstreet

To smell the ocean breeze.

To give someone a chance, then Tanner has done his job.

To recognize the beauty in everything.

To give people a chance.

To reserve judgment.

To treat everyone as you would want to be treated.

To smile at a stranger.

To say hello to someone you might have ignored.

To pick up the phone and call an old friend.

To stand up and protect those who need your help.

To not be perfect.

To enjoy the moments.

To be kind.

To be nice.

To allow yourself to love.

To live life to the fullest, then Tanner has done his job.

Your sweet woman loves you my baby boy...your sweet woman loves you...always and forever.

So, that was my speech.

Tanner's funeral was something I will always remember. Every moment of it. I took it all in. One hundred percent of it... all in. I never want to forget a thing.

As Tanner's coffin was carried out of the room, "My Hero" by the Foo Fighters played. It rocked the house. "There goes My Hero...watch him as he goes."

And then on that day...something happened that we would never forget...the Rainbow Around The Sun.

The rainbow around the sun was truly one of the most amazing moments I have ever experienced. The events that led up to the rainbow around the sun made it even more amazing.

After the service, a limousine took us up to the gravesite. Everyone followed by foot. To look out the back window of the limousine and see the sea of people walking up the hill for Tanner...it was just incredible. Simply beautiful. Simply breathtaking. The limousine parked near Tanner's grave, and I remember thinking to myself, 'Do I need my phone?' I take my phone everywhere, but I knew I didn't need it. Why would I need it? Everyone I knew was here with me. So I left the phone in the back seat.

Throughout that morning, I had this thought that I had to remember to kiss Tanner's coffin, before it was lowered into the ground. I had to remember this. And I didn't. I forgot.

After the coffin was lowered into the ground, the rabbi started to speak. I suddenly remembered what I had forgotten to do. I turned to Michael and told him. I said I had to kiss the coffin. It was already lowered in the ground, but that wasn't good enough for me. One of the rabbi's noticed I was in a sudden panic and asked Michael about it, and so he told him. We stopped everything... stopped the service, stopped it all, so I could do what I needed to do.

The ground next to the open hole, where Tanner's coffin was now six feet down, was covered in artificial turf. I got down on my stomach, with Michael holding my legs. I didn't care if my funeral dress got dirty. I didn't care if I fell in that hole. I had to do what I had to do. The rabbi told Michael not to let go, and he held onto my feet with all of his might. I kissed my hand and leaned in as far as I could. I touched the coffin with my hand. I did what I needed to do.

I got up, brushed myself off and went back to my seat.

Several minutes later, the service concluded, and everyone lined up at the grave to shovel in dirt and throw in flowers. I was the first. As people waited in line, our friends greeted us with hugs, love and words of sympathy, support and compassion.

I was talking to my dear friend Adam, when I suddenly heard a commotion. Other friends yelled for me to look up. And there, up in the sky, right before our eyes, was the rainbow around the sun. I looked around for my phone to capture the moment and remembered I had chosen to leave it behind, in the car. I remember telling everyone to take pictures and send them to me.

It was a perfect day, weather wise. The sky was blue. Hardly a cloud in the sky. If you were a mile away you might not have seen this phenomenon. The timing was perfect. Hundreds of people were at the gravesite. I had just kissed his coffin. Our friends and family were paying their respects. It was breathtaking. It made non-believers into believers. It stopped everyone in their tracks. It was life changing. It was the perfect moment for the rainbow around the sun.

I was later told this is called a sunbow or whirling rainbow. It is considered to be a sign from the creator, marking a time of great change or transition on the earth. I think it was a message from Tanner. It had to be. It was him saying, "Mommy, I'm okay." It was his way of saying, "I love you." That was Tanner.

Back in the limousine, we all looked at our phones, and what we saw was incredible. From Facebook to Instagram, everyone was posting pictures and writing about what they just witnessed, what they experienced, what they saw. Everyone was posting about the day, and their words just touched our hearts.

We had a big luncheon in Tanner's honor. Alyson and Diane did the most amazing job. Everything was perfect. A true celebration of his life.

I walked around the room and spoke to everyone. Shared with everyone. There were hundreds of people at Tanner's luncheon. From family and friends who flew in just for the day (from places like San Francisco, Seattle, Kansas City, Chicago and Philadelphia), to my ex-boyfriends and old friends, to Casey's classmates and Tanner's teachers, even people I didn't know and was meeting for the first time. It truly was a celebration of his life.

I kept a smile on my face. Inside, my heart was broken. My baby boy was not by my side. What a strange experience that was…surreal. Usually, at social gatherings, I would be wondering where Tanner was and if he was getting into trouble. This was the first time ever that I didn't have to do that. This was the new life that I would have to get used to. He was not here. I would not be watching over him anymore. How strange that was.

5.22.13

The day after...

Tanner has passed. The funeral was over. Now what? Does the "new normal" start today? I hate that saying...ugh...the new normal. Fuck that. Normal doesn't exist anymore.

An ex-boyfriend of mine texted me after the funeral. He lives back East and watched the funeral on the live stream. He listened to my speech and commented on the thing I said about never wanting to be "that" person. His text to me: "I promise never to look at you in a way, other than how I've always looked at you, which is just a pure and amazing woman." That touched my heart. I don't know, if I have ever told him how much that meant to me, and how I think about what he said to me...often. Days when I feel like I'm being looked at as "that" person...it is his words that make me feel better.

I can't believe my son is not here. I can't believe my son is under the dirt, in a box, in the ground. Who was keeping him warm at night? Who was taking care of him? He is all alone...so am I.

5.25.13

Today was Tanner's half birthday. He would have been eleven and a half. We celebrated him, by making pancakes and watching the brand-new *SpongeBob* episode.

We all still couldn't get over the rainbow around the sun. It was talked about again and again. It was just so amazing. So calming. So incredible.

One week without our sweet boy. We were still numb…still in shock over the loss. We missed him more than words can say.

5.31.13

It had now been just about two weeks since Tanner died. My heart was broken…it is broken. But I was still getting up every morning. I was still going about my day. I was still working, functioning, breathing…doing what I had to do…being a mother, a daughter, a girlfriend, a friend.

I was also thinking about some things that happened over the past few weeks.

The day Tanner died, when we had our house filled with friends and family, a friend of mine handed me some pills, "You're going to need these," she said. I put them in a drawer. I had no idea what they were…anxiety pills? Sleeping pills? I had never taken drugs, and I was not going to start now. I wasn't mad that she did that. She meant well. And for many others, those pills would have been welcomed. Just not for me. I wanted to feel every feeling. I wanted to remember each thought and emotion.

Also on that day, a family member took me aside and said, "What are you doing? You should be upstairs with your bedroom door closed." I was told I "shouldn't be" downstairs talking with my family and friends. Really? Maybe that's what *they* would have done. But that's not me. No one should tell anyone, especially at a time like this, what they *should* be doing? There are no rules. You do what you want to do and you do what feels right. I was not going to hide anywhere.

Everybody handles tragedy and loss differently. That I know. Where one would walk, another would run. I was going to face this full on, head on. That's who I am. And that's what I did.

June 2013

Life without Tanner. How difficult that is to say. The house was quiet. Our lives were quiet. His presence was so missed.

Packages still came for him. He had placed "pre-orders" on some DVD's and so his deliveries continued to arrive. The Fed Ex person, the UPS person (who we knew by name, Debra), the USPS person...they all knew Tanner had passed away. They looked at me with sad eyes.

This was the month of "getting used to." Getting used to him not being here. Getting used to a new schedule.

Three weeks after Tanner passed away, Casey graduated from middle school. I bought her a bouquet of flowers, and I placed it on a chair during the ceremony. Towards the end, I noticed a bee was just chilling in the flowers. A woman sitting next to me said the bee has been there the whole time. For one and a half hours, the bee calmly sat in the flowers as Casey graduated. After the ceremony, before I could give her the flowers, the bee flew away. The bee didn't scare me (and bees usually scare me!) or show any aggression. It was just calm. I took it all in. It was more than a bee to me.

I had a dream. I was in a restaurant that was at the top of a hotel. I was holding Tanner's hand, but I didn't realize I was holding his hand, nor did I realize he was with me. A bartender told me to be careful...it was crowded and dark. I told him we were just looking for someone and would leave soon. I saw a few familiar faces. I heard someone call out my name. I wondered if they all knew that Tanner had passed away.

We headed out and as we got to the stairs it occurred to me that Tanner was by my side. He didn't say anything to me, but I leaned down to him and started kissing him. I felt his cheeks. I felt his warmth. I realized I was with him, but also that he had passed away. I yelled out, "It's like *The Time Travelers Wife*. It's like *The Time Traveler's Wife*." I was happy because I realized that I could kiss and feel him again, because we could time travel to each other. My alarm clock woke me up from the dream...it was "SexyBack" playing...Tanner's ring tone.

Greg finally had his surgery...the surgery he was supposed to have the day Tanner died. Thankfully, everything went well.

His colon was removed successfully, and there was absolutely no signs of cancer.

The end of June. Casey decided to go to overnight camp for a month. I wouldn't be selfish. Of course she should go. But what about me? How would I handle being in the house all alone? It was too soon. It was too scary. It was too sad. I had no choice. I had had no choice with any of this. I needed to keep busy. To keep sane. Casey needed to live. I needed to survive.

I planned a five-day trip with Michael in July…up the California coast. It would be nice to get away…it had been so long. But at the same time, I feared leaving. I didn't like this "getting used to."

July 2013

I had another incredible dream. I was in line in a bathroom and I heard Tanner's voice. I saw him. He was wearing a red long sleeve shirt and jeans...his usual outfit before he got sick. "Mommy!" he yelled to me. I asked him, "What are you doing here?" "I'm keeping you company while you wait in line," he replied. Such a simple dream, but it meant so much to me. It feels so good to have dreams that seem so real. I have had a few, and I hoped this was just the beginning of more "real" Tanner dreams.

Casey was at camp, and Michael and I would be leaving in about a week for our trip up the coast. I had a few days before we left to do whatever I wanted to do.

I drove to Newport Beach. I saw friends. I stayed in a beautiful room at Pelican Hill. I drank wine. I ate dessert. I watched the sunset. I listened to Dave Matthews Band. I forgot my reality... just for a little bit. It was just what I needed...so amazing, so close to perfect.

Fourth of July came and went. It is Greg's birthday. The first without Tanner. Tanner was not a fan of this holiday. He hated fireworks. Scared of them. Scared of the noise, the loud booms. It was the first holiday in a long time when I didn't have little ears to cover. I watched the beautiful colors in the sky with tears in my eyes. Life would never be the same again.

Michael and I drove up the coast to Morro Bay, Big Sur and Napa. A well-deserved vacation, but a sad one. Moments of happiness, yes, but it was tough. Nothing would be easy anymore. I realized getting away was nice, but you can never actually "get away." You can't escape the sadness, the reality, the tragedy. It follows you wherever you go. Even to paradise.

It was almost two months since Tanner died. I kept looking out for signs, messages, anything from him. Because, *what if?* What if he *were* trying to reach me? If there is *even* the slightest, smallest possibility? *What if?* So everywhere I went, I looked for signs from Tanner. And, on this trip, I definitely had a sign.

I have a favorite Sydney Evan ring that I wear. It's white gold and says "love" in diamonds. I bought it a few years ago when I was in Aspen with an ex-boyfriend. It was a purchase I made for myself...as a divorced, independent woman.

Rainbow Around The Son

As Michael and I drove up the coast, I remember playing with my love ring. Switching it back and forth, from one finger to the other. It's a nervous habit I have.

We decided to stop and see the elephant seals. I walked along the edge of the rocks…taking pictures, talking to Tanner. Thinking about life. After a while, I went back to the car, sat down and looked down at my hand. My love ring was gone.

I searched the entire car – the seats, the floor. It wasn't there. I thought maybe it might have fallen off while I was outside. I got out of the car and started walking the route I had taken, back and forth, back and forth. As I searched and searched, I talked to Tanner. I told him to help me, to lead me to the ring. Nothing. I got back to the car. Very upset. My ring was nowhere to be found.

The next morning, in Big Sur, I woke up early in our hotel room. I hadn't yet unpacked from the day before, so I started to take all of my clothes out of my suitcase. I reached for a black tank top at the bottom. It was rolled up just as I had packed it three days earlier. I hadn't touched it nor worn it yet. I took it out and heard a clank. My love ring. It fell out of the shirt and onto the floor. I gasped. I stared at it. It had to be Tanner. The ring means even more to me now.

August 2013

I now had a high-schooler. Casey was a freshman. Routines began. Time didn't stop. It moved forward...whether I liked it or not. I didn't write every day as I used to. I just couldn't. I didn't have it in me. Instead, I threw myself into work. Into Casey. Into starting a Foundation. Into my new life.

Every week I went to the cemetery and always had fresh flowers in hand. You know when you have company coming over to your house, and you want to make sure your home is in order and clean? That's how I felt about the cemetery. I knew other people, besides me, visited Tanner. And so it was important to me that his grave always looked its best. Fresh flowers are a must...always.

I had lunch with a friend and a crazy thing happened on the way home today...

One of my favorite things to do with Tanner was to watch, *Diners, Drive-ins and Dives*, Guy Fieri's show. We would watch it late at night and say "ewww" over the gross food and "yum" over the good stuff. Since Tanner's death, I have looked for little signs: coincidences, signals, messages. Today when I was driving home, I took a street I never had driven down before...and there was Guy Fieri standing there...filming a commercial in our neighborhood. I stopped my car to talk to him and told him all about Tanner. I told Guy what an incredible, brave, funny kid Tanner was and how much we loved watching *Diners, Drive-ins and Dives* together. I told him about Casey, and he asked me to get her from home and bring her back so he could meet her. I remember thinking how I wished Tanner had been there to experience something so cool. But then again, I think that's why we met Guy. I think Tanner planned the whole thing.

September 2013

It was the one-year anniversary since my life changed. I posted about it on Facebook.

Today sucked. Actually, every day sucked. But today really sucked. For the past year, every day, I would think: a year ago today everything was okay...this time, one year ago, we were okay. But after today, I couldn't do that anymore. This time last year it was not okay.

This was not an anniversary to celebrate. A year ago today our life changed. Forever. A year ago today we walked into the hospital thinking our son had a flu, a virus, meningitis, something he would recover from. It had been one year, since an emergency room doctor walked in the room, closed the door and told us to sit down.

One year since words like brain tumor, edema, cancer and glioblastoma began to work their way into our daily language.

After that day, we were blessed (is that even the right word?) to have eight months and eight days more with Tanner. Eight months and eight days. That's 250 days. I didn't know what to say about that. Two hundred and fifty days. I guess I can say we were fortunate to have 250 and not 249, but why not 251? Three hundred? Why did we even have to be put in a situation where we were given "days"?

Yes, this is a hard week, but this past weekend was a weekend I had been looking forward to...for a very long time. It was my Dave Matthews Band concert weekend.

You know when there's something that just clicks with you... something you just get lost in? It may sound cheesy, but that's what Dave Matthews Band is to me. Years ago, several very special people in my life shared with me their love for Dave, and their enthusiasm caught on with me. "Crash Into Me." "Crush." "The Space Between." "The Stone." "Seek Up." "You and Me." "Grey Street." "If I Had It All." Too many favorite songs to even mention, but those were my songs. The lyrics speak to me. And then last year, right before Tanner got sick, it was all about "#41." It became my ring tone. It became my song.

Last year, I had tickets to see Dave Matthews Band, but never made it, since that was the weekend Tanner got sick. It was "#41" that rang and rang on my phone, while we sat at the hospital.

"#41" suddenly had a whole new meaning. That music became my *SpongeBob*. As much as Tanner loved his cartoons, I fell more and more into my Dave Matthews music. It was my escape. Sometimes, late at night, when Tanner would watch his cartoons, I would put on my headphones and drift off listening to Dave. Tanner would say, "Mommy, why are you listening to your music?" I would tell him because Mommy loved these songs. It made Mommy happy… and he would smile.

Last Friday night at the Chula Vista show, Dave Matthews sang "#41." I felt like I was the only one there, and that he was singing that song just for me.

So you see, Dave Matthews and his music had a whole new meaning for me. Should I change my ringtone, since it reminded me of that time? I can't. Because Tanner knew it was my ringtone… my song, and he got to know it, too.

Look, life goes on. It just does. Babies are being born. Celebrations still happen. We just had to adjust to every day being another day without our guy. Every morning I got up. I got out of bed. On the outside, I was keeping it together. But on the inside? I felt incomplete, as though a part of my heart was gone. That smile you see in my pictures? It is a smile for the moment, but not a real honest-to-goodness smile. I've had just a few of those because truthfully, part of that smile is gone. I'm angry. I'm sad.

Marlo Gottfurcht Longstreet

The emotions come in *waves*. It is the only way I can describe it. Waves. Sometimes small. Sometimes big. Sometimes very big. One minute I am okay. The next I am not. That is my life now. I miss my son.

Slowly but surely we were getting back to life. I've gone out with my friends. Shared a few bottles of my favorite Prisoner wine with some special people. I've laughed. I've cried. You know, that saying, how life is short, and you only live once? I can attest to that. I live it. I don't have time for drama. For gossip. For bullshit. I just wanted to be with the ones I really wanted to be with. It should be that simple. But it wasn't. I wish it were. I'm really trying here. But honestly, it all just sucks.

So what now? We were starting our Foundation in Tanner's name. That was my purpose now. To spread the gospel of Tanner. What else am I supposed to do for a kid who brings us a rainbow around the sun? This is what I was meant to do. It was what I was focused on every day, and we've only just begun. It is a process. It is emotional. It is hard. It takes time. One foot in front of the other. That's what I was doing. That, and being a Mom to my beautiful dancing daughter, Casey. One day at a time.

Today was the day I had been dreading. Today was the first day when I couldn't say things were okay this time last year. Today marked the day when the nightmare began, and continues still.

Rainbow Around The Son

It has been almost four months since Tanner was gone...115 days if you were counting...and I was.

October 2013

It was Sunday night. The house was quiet and my thoughts were brewing.

How do I respond when someone asks me how many kids I have? This happened twice this week. "Two," I say...because I will always have two. One woman who asked in casual conversation cried when I told her my story. The other woman was asking so that she could give me enough Halloween candy to bring home to my kids. What do I say? The truth...the truth is, it is just all really messed up. No matter what, I will always have two kids.

Was it getting easier? Nope. Actually, just the opposite. Harder. Maybe because it had been five months. Maybe because the shock was wearing off. Maybe because everyone just goes back to their lives and daily routines, and I just go day in and day out, hour by hour, moment by moment, second by second without Tanner. Maybe it was because his birthday was coming up, Casey's birthday was coming up. Halloween. Thanksgiving. Christmas.

The time of year I always loved, always looked forward to. It was different now, and it would never be the same again.

So there I sat...thinking about it all. I thank those who have been wonderful and loving and supportive. I thank those who have been patient and understanding, and who know that I am not the same social butterfly that I used to be. I thank those who have listened to me...through my thoughts and tears. I thank those who didn't know what to say to me, but still say something. I thank those who didn't hide from me, didn't ignore me, didn't pretend they didn't see me just because they didn't know what to say.

I struggled with those who hadn't said a word. How can someone be a part of your life, someone you have known for years (whether you keep in touch or not), and that person doesn't say a word? I just don't get it. I know, I know...some people just don't know what to say. I know I live every parent's worst nightmare. But does that mean you don't acknowledge the loss? There may be no words, you may not have the right words, but just a squeeze, a hug, a smile, a check-in, an email, a text, a card, a call...anything. Even if you say, "I just don't know what to say," you're still saying *something*. It doesn't take a lot of effort in this day and age, but a little effort goes a long way.

On the outside, I did my thing. On the inside, I was under my covers curled up in a ball. I did my thing for Casey...she is my everything. I embraced those closest to me, my closest friends, who texted and called daily and made sure I was breathing my next breath.

When I close my eyes I see my baby. I see Tanner's big brown eyes and his goofy smile. I hear him, his laughter, his calling me "Mommy" and saying "I love you." I feel him...all the time. He is here...with me...as he has always been and always will be.

I visited the cemetery often and always brought fresh flowers. I talked to him...everywhere. I called out taxi numbers and elevator brands. Sometimes I accidently called the dog, Tanner. Sometimes I accidently called Casey, Tanner. Sometimes I just get in my car and drive to...nowhere. Sometimes I run and run until I was out of breath. Sometimes I walked on the beach and watched the pelicans dive in the water and cried my eyes out. Sometimes I sang out loud, "there must be some kind of way out of here said the joker to the thief." Honestly? I just wanted to take my shoes off, feel the blades of grass between my toes, dance, love and dream of a time that made me smile. A time when I was ME.

I didn't know what tomorrow or next week would be like. Or next month. Or next year. I just took it one day at a time. I couldn't really plan for tomorrow because, as I had learned, my tomorrows were taken away.

Marlo Gottfurcht Longstreet

I missed feeling amazing...I missed the simple days of amazing.

10.25.13

My life was forever different. I was no longer the soccer mom. I was the mom trying to figure out what the hell was happening, dealing with my son's death and making sure my daughter stayed healthy.

My dad and I worked daily on our Foundation, which we name: Tanner Project Foundation. We researched. We talked to experts. We met with doctors and scientists. Every day we learned more and more about the mutant p53 gene.

The p53 gene is the biggest tumor suppressor gene in our body. We get one from our mother and one from our father. It's an important gene...possibly one of the most important...because it fights cancer. Most of us have a healthy p53 gene that helps to suppress cancer. If you have a damaged p53 gene (like Tanner did, like Casey and Greg do), it can cause cell mutation, which means cancer. The p53 gene is one of the master switches for cancer... it is that important.

If you have a mutant p53 gene and more than one cancer in your family, you have what is known as Li-Fraumeni Syndrome (LFS). Having the mutated gene greatly increases the risk of developing many different cancers during one's lifetime, including:

brain, breast, blood, bone, soft-tissue sarcoma, adrenal cortical, colon and melanoma, to name a few.

What we are learning is that the mutated gene is rare. My thoughts? Maybe it was only rare because people didn't know about it and didn't know to test for it. Can't be that rare if our family had it. There was so much current information about the BRCA gene...not much information about the mutant p53. I just didn't get it.

So, on this fall October day, my dad, Michael and I are off to Boston. My dad and I will be attending the Li-Fraumeni Syndrome Symposium. Doctors from around the world would be in one room, at Dana-Farber Cancer Institute, talking about the thing that has changed my life. It is here I would learn so much. It is here I would ask questions. It is here I would make new contacts. It is here I would find out the leaders in the field and what advances are being made. It is here I would meet other families that were like ours...who had suffered loss and were going through disease. It is here I would learn we are not alone.

10.30.13

The most amazing thing happened to us the other night.

Thanks to our friend Georgianna, we had the opportunity to meet Dave Grohl, lead singer of the Foo Fighters, at a charity event. We told him how we played "My Hero" at Tanner's funeral. He was taken aback. Not that we used the song, but that we used the real version. The rock version. "You didn't use the acoustic one?" he asked. "No," we said. He couldn't believe it. We told him how powerful it was to hear "My Hero" play as we walked down the aisle with Tanner's coffin. No other song would have played it so appropriate, so perfect.

We shared our story with him. I cried to him. He put his hand on my head, soothing me, as he listened to me cry about Tanner.

"My Hero" is such a compelling song. And we talked about how everyone has their own interpretation of the song. There are thousands of them. Hundreds of thousands of them. When he wrote that song, he had something particular in mind. When we listen to that song, we each think of something totally different. That's the beauty of music and lyrics and creativity and imagination and individuality.

Later that night, Dave Grohl took the stage, and we recorded him as he played. After several songs, he strummed his guitar and started to speak to the crowd.

"...I meet people every once in a while that come up to me and they say, 'Hey man, this song means a lot to me for this specific reason.' And I just had this conversation with a couple people right here [he was referring to us!] and you

know a lot of these songs, like I will write them on a fucking napkin in my basement and then I turn them into a song. And then I go into a studio and I record it. And every night I get to go sing it to a bunch of people for my reason, but then they sing it back to me for like 80,000 different reasons. And it's one of the greatest things about being a musician is that I get to look out at you guys, and I get to see myself and I hope that you get to look at me and see yourself as well. So this one goes out to all of the people that I talked to tonight [us again!]. It's called My Hero."

It was the acoustic version…and he sang it for us.

Sigh…

November 2013

November...the beginning of the month I had been dreading. Yes, it was Casey's birthday, but it was also Tanner's birthday and Thanksgiving...the first without him.

Tonight, the first night of November, I sat by the fire with a glass of red wine. I was alone so I took this moment to go on Facebook and read all my friends' comments after my last post, and the post before that and the post before that.

I was overwhelmed by the responses. I am told, again and again, how inspiring my words are. I write from my heart. I write when I feel the need. I don't write to get likes or comments. I write because at that moment it's what I feel and I feel like sharing.

What amazed me tonight, as I read through the comments, are the people in my life: family of course; childhood friends; friends from summer camp; friends from elementary school, high school and college; sorority sisters and friends I had worked with; baby class friends and friends I met in the waiting room at Tanner's various therapies; Tanner's teachers, who had become my friends and friends I had met because our kids went to the same school; siblings and families of friends; friends of friends; dance mom friends and Casey's and Greg's friends; friends I haven't seen in twenty years; life-long friends and best friends. Never could I imagine that someone I met at sleep away camp in 1985 would fly cross-country to Tanner's funeral (thank you Magen). Never could I imagine that my third grade best friend, who I haven't seen since third grade but who, when we reconnected on Facebook, would send me messages of support (thank you Sarah). Say what you want about social media…Facebook has been a blessing to me. To know so many people cared, so many people from all stages of my life…it gives me strength and touches my heart. Thank you all.

11.20.13

Casey turned fifteen today.

I thought back to where we were a year ago. In the hospital for those ten days. And now here we are. This birthday was so bittersweet. Casey and Tanner celebrated together. It was *their* birthday month. Now she celebrated alone.

Casey is forever changed. We all are. She is beyond her years. She has experienced more in the past fourteen months than most people experience in a lifetime. With all that she had gone through...all that she goes through...she is extraordinary. She smiles. She is happy. She laughs. She has fun. She dances. She communicates. She excels. She is social. She is everything so many people couldn't be after losing a sibling and knowing you also have this cancer gene.

Last year she couldn't have a party. This year I insisted she have one. She invited thirty friends to Benihana. We celebrated her...she so deserved that and more.

11.25.13

Today was Tanner's birthday. The first without him. He would have been twelve.

In our home we have a funny doorbell. It plays different tunes. When we first got it, the kids thought it was hilarious. Sometimes it played "Take Me Out To The Ballgame," and sometimes it was "Jingle Bells." Yesterday, Greg rang the doorbell...and it played "Happy Birthday." I hadn't heard it play "Happy Birthday" in, I don't know how long. In fact, now that I think about it, I hadn't even known it played "Happy Birthday." But that's what was playing, and how appropriate it was.

The six months between Tanner's eleventh birthday and the day he passed, we made sure every day was like a birthday. There might not have been candles to blow out, but presents and deliveries and celebrating and kisses and love were what we did every day. We didn't look at the day on the calendar. We just celebrated our brave boy...daily.

But today is that day. November 25. And this year we celebrated Tanner's twelfth birthday...without him.

On this day, I thought back to the day he was born, twelve years ago, at 10:06 a.m. My baby, weighing in at eight pounds, four ounces and ten days early. Dark hair, dark eyes. My little guy who was, in fact, not so little. He was such a boy...a linebacker... not dainty like Casey at all. This big, mushy boy was mine, and he won my heart.

The love between us was so strong, so familiar, as if we knew had known each other, as if we had this connection from another lifetime. He was a tough kid, not easy at all, but with all that came love, so much of it.

So today we celebrated my guy. The boy who brought us a rainbow around the sun. The boy who had touched so many lives. He was so very missed. His presence was as big as he was little. There were truly no words to describe our loss.

Today our doorbell will ring "Happy Birthday." Today we will eat Tanner's favorite food. Today we will enjoy his favorite dessert. Today we will blow out his candles. Today we will be together, as a family, because family is what he loved the most. Today we will remember. Today we will celebrate Tanner...a boy we all miss... and love...so very much.

Happy Birthday Tanner.

11.28.13

Thanksgiving. Our first without Tanner.

For the past few months, I had been thinking about this day... about Thanksgiving. What would make me feel somewhat okay with today? Being with my family was most important.

We went to a hotel for dinner. I had no appetite. Tanner should have been with us. He wouldn't have loved it...that's the truth... but he would have been there. He would have sat in his chair, with his iPhone or iPad, headphones on and complained about everything. He would have asked every five minutes when we were going to go home. I would have given anything to hear his complaints. But there we were...all sad. All missing Tanner.

December 2013

We began December as we had faced November. We got through the birthday month and Thanksgiving. Now we just have to get through the holidays and New Year (and of course my birthday in January). One moment at a time.

We were still very private and protective about Casey's diagnosis of having the mutant p53 gene. Many people asked about her, but we kept her privacy sacred. We really didn't want people to know, until she was ready for people to know. Time still needed to pass…between Tanner's illness and death, and people knowing she carried the same gene.

I was also consumed with Casey's health. Making sure every cough was just that…a cough. That every headache was just that…a headache. Not reading into every ailment. Not "going there," when I didn't need to. I needed to be levelheaded about Casey. Let her live her life and not think that every step she took would cause her to fall. Easier said than done.

Marlo Gottfurcht Longstreet

12.9.13

When I met Michael, we were just friends. Single parents with kids. I don't know how it actually started, but Tuesday night family dinners became our "thing." Every Tuesday night we would have dinner together. He and his girls, Katie and Emily, and us.

Sometimes we would go to his home, push his couches together, and everyone would do their homework. Sometimes they would come over to our home, to hang out, and we would order in or cook dinner. Sometimes we would just go out to a restaurant. Regardless of what we did, Tuesday nights was our night…until things changed.

Tuesday nights were just a memory after Tanner got sick. Things would never be the same again. Our family outings would never be the same. Honestly. It would no longer be a table for six… it was just five now. And that was hard.

It was Michael's daughter, Emily's, tenth birthday, and we were planning a dinner to celebrate. We decided to go to the Century City Mall. We went to one restaurant for appetizers and another for dinner. Afterwards, we went to the Vanilla Bake Shop for dessert.

You know those signs I have talked about…signs I look for, that mean so much to me? The rainbow around the sun. My love ring getting lost then found. My Tanner dreams. I constantly kept my eyes open for the signs. But something extraordinary happened that night, the night of Emily's birthday dinner. Something that was right up there with the rainbow around the sun. Something so powerful.

We were in the Vanilla Bake Shop getting cupcakes for dessert, and across from the shop was a Tesla store. And, sitting between the Tesla store and the bakery, on the pedestrian pathway, sat a Tesla car. (Tanner loved Tesla's. When he was alive, we often went into the stores. At the time, you rarely saw one on the road. Now, in Los Angeles, they are everywhere.)

We were the only ones in the Vanilla Bake Shop...just our family. We were at the register, which is at the end of the shop. Across from us were the glass windows and door that led out to the mall.

I looked up at the glass windows and door. We should have seen our reflection in the window, but what I saw surprised me. I didn't see the five of us. I saw an image that looked like Tanner. It confused me. I told Casey to grab her phone and take a picture. So she did.

I had forgotten all about that moment, but two nights later I suddenly remembered. I asked Casey about the picture. She said, "Mom, you're not going to believe it."

Marlo Gottfurcht Longstreet

I looked at the picture and was speechless. There are no words to describe what I saw staring back at me.

Do you see what I see? What everyone sees when I show them this picture? No...your eyes are not playing tricks on you. It's Tanner. Who else could it be?

I truly think that this was a moment that wasn't supposed to be captured, yet we captured it. What other explanation is there? It was Tanner. No doubt about it. That was him. Smiling right at us. Arm on the Tesla. It was him. Like the rainbow around the sun, that was Tanner saying he was okay.

12.22.13

My friend's daughter died of cancer. The friend I had met through this journey, the mom who had already lost her son. Both of her children had the mutant p53 gene, and now she had lost both of them. My biggest nightmare. No words. Absolutely heartbreaking.

12.31.13

Tomorrow was a New Year. A new beginning. It was supposed to be a good thing. But is it? A new year...2014. All it meant to me was a year that Tanner would never experience. A year he would never write down on a piece of paper. A year he would never live in. Leaving behind 2013 meant leaving behind the last year that he lived, had experienced life and breathed. A new year meant a new year without Tanner. Happy Fucking New Year.

January 2014

I took Casey to the hospital for her annual MRI. As I drove, she turned to me and said, "Mommy, I'm getting my scans today and they may show I'm okay, but what about tomorrow? What if cancer happens tomorrow? Do we have to wait a whole year for scans to see the cancer?" I didn't have an answer. She was right.

After a long day at the hospital where Casey had her scans, I got home and thought back to what she said. With the mutant p53 gene, there is a surveillance protocol we follow that doctors have suggested for people who carry this mutated gene. So, we do what we are told. But is this enough?

I told my dad about my conversation with Casey that morning. Although we thought about this before, it was in that moment that we truly understood what we needed to focus on. We would not "follow the rules" of the standard protocol. Yes, we could make it our baseline, but we also needed to think way outside the box. We needed to do more.

My dad is a very laser-focused kind of guy. And when he takes on a project, no stone is left unturned. So we shifted gears and made it our number one priority to find someone who could help us keep Casey, and others, healthy.

We had already met so many experts, throughout the country, both in the medical and research communities. We asked them to work on a project with us, which we would fund, to monitor Casey every day, not the standard protocol of every year. Everyone understood what we were saying, yet no one seemed to want to help us.

We were finally referred to a researcher, who we heard might be able to take on this project.

1.16.14

Dr. Nicholas Schork worked at the J. Craig Venter Institute (JCVI) in La Jolla, California, a beautiful beach town just north of San Diego. Dr. Craig Venter led the first team to sequence the human genome, and JCVI is a world leader in genomic research.

The J. Craig Venter Institute is a building, unlike anything I had ever seen. Located across from University of California, San Diego, the building is architecturally beautiful, and is also the first net-zero energy carbon-neutral biological lab of its kind. We met with Dr. Schork (whom we are now told to call "Nik") in a conference room, since his office had not yet been set up following his move from Scripps to JCVI.

I told Nik my story. About Tanner. About Casey. We told him about our Foundation, and that we would fund a project to keep Casey healthy: to do more than the typical protocol, to think outside the box in order to catch disease before it becomes disease. I told him about Casey asking me what happens if cancer happens tomorrow. We told him we don't have tomorrows...we know that because of Tanner. We told him that we had talked to numerous doctors, researchers and scientists, and we couldn't find anyone to help us keep Casey healthy, beyond following the standard protocol. We spoke and he listened. After a while, he looked at us with a smile.

Nik told us that one of the main reasons he came to JCVI was to work on N-of-1 studies. That's the study of one. You study one person, and what you learn from that one person, can eventually help others who have the same or similar medical profile. My dad and I looked at each other. We had no idea that what we wanted, in order to help Casey and others, had a name: N-of-1.

Sitting there, telling our story, while Nik listened intently... it all fell into place in that conference room. Nik said he would work with us, and Casey would be the N-of-1. For the first time, I felt like we might just have a handle on this.

February 2014

Presidents Day Weekend came and went. It was another dance competition weekend with Casey at Disneyland. I remembered last year like it was yesterday.

You know what one of the hardest things for me was now? It was being able to go to events, like a dance competition for the weekend and not having to worry about Tanner. It was this mixture of guilt and relief. Casey had sacrificed so much for so many years...not just when he was sick. Finally, finally...it was all about her. We could stay at Disneyland for as long as we wanted. We could jump in the car, on an airplane, on a train...and not have to worry. So bittersweet to have these mixed emotions.

It has now been over a month since we started working with Nik and JCVI. We have had meeting after meeting after meeting. Nik brought in his colleagues, and now the Tanner Project had a "team" that was diligently working on the N-of-1 study.

The bottom line, remember, is to "catch cancer before it becomes cancer." Stage 0. Our research goal was clear: with Casey being the N-of-1, and since she has an over 90% chance of getting cancer, is there something about Casey that Nik and our team can learn to protect her and eventually others?

The standard protocol, for those with the mutant p53 gene, is to have an MRI (brain and body) once a year, as well as quarterly ultrasounds of the abdomen and pelvis and blood work. We would continue these tests, but amp it up. Do more and more often.

The most important aspect for the N-of-1 was not to interfere with Casey's life. How could we make the testing work to fit into her schedule? How could we do it non-invasively? Nik, along with Dr. Laura Goetz and Dr. Victoria (Vicki) Magnuson, worked out a protocol and schedule which would be convenient and acceptable to everyone.

Typically, Casey would have her blood taken every three months; now they wanted it done once a month. This would be hard for her...to go to a lab once a month. So, for her blood assays, we would get a mobile phlebotomist to collect her blood at home, who would then send in her samples. The rule was simple...nothing could interfere with Casey's life. The N-of-1 would simply work around it.

March 2014

My dad came up with an idea. Why don't we make a movie? A fifteen-minute short video, kind of like a documentary, about the Tanner Project? It would be about our journey...both personally and medically.

We talked about what we wanted this movie to be, and we knew it had to address everything...what happened with Tanner, our future with Casey (and her having the mutant p53 gene) and our collaboration with Nik and the J. Craig Venter Institute.

The movie would be a very private and personal one. It would not be broadcast on the internet. It would not be sent out in emails. It would only be shown when we were present - to doctors, researchers and scientists, as well as to our family and friends.

We knew this movie would be something important. We just had to make sure it was done right. Since it was so personal, it was going to be a difficult and sensitive process. I knew whoever was going to help us had to be someone I trusted.

Claudio. He was the perfect person. Not only is he a great, lifelong friend (who was there for us during Tanner's illness and death), he is also CEO, Founder/President and Chief Creative Officer of CG Creative Studios. CG Creative is a creative communications agency that does brand strategy, creative development and also designs and produces corporate events worldwide. Claudio is one of the most talented and creative people I know. I was certain that he and his team should be the ones to help us create and produce our movie.

Throughout this process…establishing the Tanner Project Foundation, collaborating with people like Nik…everything just fell into place. And, coincidentally, CG Creative's offices were also in La Jolla, just a ten minute drive from the J. Craig Venter Institute.

3.5.14

My dad and I drove down to La Jolla to meet Claudio and his team at the CG Creative offices.

We explained our vision to the team…our journey with Tanner, Casey, JCVI and the Tanner Project. My dad suggested we might need a celebrity, a "name," to star in our movie and tell our story. Claudio had to step out of our meeting to take a phone call, so we continued to brainstorm without him.

A little while later, Claudio came back into the room. Without hesitating and without knowing what we had discussed, he sat down and simply said, "We don't need a name. We have Marlo."

We all looked at him. It was true...and he was right. Who better to tell my story the way it was supposed to be told...but me.

3.13.14

Casey danced her solo this weekend. She dedicated her performance to Tanner. Her solo was to "Beautiful Freak" - another song that was played at the funeral. She wore a red flower in her hair. Red was Tanner's favorite color.

3.24.14

It had been so great to work with my dad on this project. We have always been very close...he has always been by my side, and I by his. It was his help, his guidance, his brilliance, his support that made the Tanner Project possible.

We continued with the plans for our movie with CG Creative. My dad and I wrote the script (I guess this is where my college major in screenwriting came in handy). We wrote, we rewrote; we wanted every word to be perfect. For the first time in a long while, I was excited about something.

April 2014

As we slowly approached the one-year anniversary of Tanner's death, I just couldn't believe how much time had passed.

I missed my boy. I missed sleeping next to him. I missed feeling him. I missed hearing him breathe in and out. I missed hearing him say "I love you" every morning. I missed his everything. I just couldn't believe it had been almost a year. I didn't know how I could go a lifetime without him.

4.13.14

We planned a family vacation. Over spring break, to Palm Desert, with Casey and I and Michael and his girls. This time two years ago, Tanner was with us in Palm Desert. This year it was different. So hard. So different.

I was sitting at the pool, and my wonderful and incredibly supportive friends, Jon and Julie, texted me. They were also in the Desert attending Coachella, the annual music festival. They heard we were in town and had two extra artist passes to that nights show. Did Casey and I want them? Of course!

So, there we were, Mama and Daughter going to our first Coachella. I saw my friends, and Casey ran into some of hers. It was an incredible experience. The highlight of the night for Casey was seeing Lana Del Rey perform. The highlight of the night for me was watching Casey see Lana Del Rey perform.

Thank you Jon and Julie for a great night. One that we needed. One that we will always remember.

4.23.14

We started filming the movie. I re-lived it all. It was an emotional experience. An emotional and compelling story and one that had to be told.

The first half was all about Tanner and his illness. Pictures of Tanner and Casey run throughout the movie as I narrated. We filmed these scenes at the cemetery and in my backyard. The second half was the scientific part...and would be filmed at the J. Craig Venter Institute.

Of what I had seen so far, the raw footage looked great. I knew the editing process, which I would be a big part of, would be an emotional one.

May 2014

The dreaded month. The one-year anniversary.

How do I even call it an anniversary? To me, an anniversary is a celebration. This was not a celebration. Remembering the day Tanner died was the last thing I wanted to celebrate. What was a better name to call it? The one-year remembrance? I was not looking forward to this month.

5.11.14

Mother's Day 2014...the first without Tanner. I thought back to last year when he gave me the best gift ever...spending the day by my side, with laughter and smiles and cuddles and love. This year as we remembered our special guy, I spent the day, of course, with my beautiful daughter.

That morning I watched Casey dance, and we had brunch with my mom. In the afternoon, we went to the Marina and got up on paddle-boards, windy day and all, for the very first time. We laughed a lot thinking Tanner was probably causing the wind… waiting to see if we would fall off the boards and into the water. We were two strong women doing our thing, and we did pretty well (and stayed dry!). The day was complete with dinner at my favorite restaurant with my family.

So many of my friends checked in today. Every message made today a little easier. I am so grateful for my wonderful friends.

5.18.14

I took Casey to get a manicure and pedicure…something… anything…to get our minds off of this one-year anniversary. It was a treat for us; and we went to a place we didn't normally go to. I noticed a woman across from me…a familiar face. Her daughter and Tanner had once been in a class together.

As I got up to pay, the woman also got up. She turned to me and said, "I recognize you from school." With a big smile on her face, she said to me, "How is your sweet boy? He was always so cute and smiling." I looked at her, very surprised, and said, "Tanner died last year. This is the one-year anniversary of his death." With tears in her eyes she said to me, "That was him?" She had heard about a classmate who was ill and had died, but never put two and two together…that that boy was Tanner. I hugged her...twice. It was a surreal moment...I was not sure how to act and react. But I took in the goodness of it.

Of all days...I was given a gift with this moment. To know someone out there had been thinking of Tanner, as alive and well and smiling and cute and happy...that felt good. She also gave me the gift of knowing how fondly she remembered Tanner.

So, here we were. A year later. A year filled with sadness, anger, resentment. A year filled with many questions and few answers. A year filled with some smiles, some laughter, many tears. A year filled with memories, stories, pictures, videos, "remember when's?" A year filled with change and acceptance. The "milestone" one-year anniversary was here...one year without Tanner.

I had been thinking a lot about what today would bring. Some people will say that a year is enough time to mourn, that it was time to move on, to get back to "normal" (whatever "normal" is). That's complete bullshit. For me, it was trying to find that "happy" place. The place of acceptance. The place that's healthy. The place that allows you to smile and laugh and have fun (and be okay with it) even when you're sad and grieving...that happy medium.

Every day I did move on. Every day I put one foot in front of the other. We moved forward each day. We missed him. We looked around and saw things that Tanner would have loved.

But now we see the world in a different way. So many times this year people told me stories of how Tanner had made a profound impact on their lives. It seemed to have started with the rainbow around the sun...that moment changed many.

Every day I have lived my life. I have tried my best. I am blessed to be a Mom to Casey....my shining light and love. I stop and smell the roses. I stay strong. I don't sweat the small stuff. I look around. I make choices for me...for my family. I realize more than ever that life is precious...a gift. Life is short but sweet for certain. Dance. Laugh. Breathe. Enjoy. Create Amazing. Viva la Vida. Make your heart smile. Knowledge is power. Take risks. Take chances. Life is scary...but spending it every day feeling unhappy and unhealthy is scarier. Spend your days with those you love... those that make you feel amazing. Do what makes you happy and complete...everything else will fall into place.

We will have an unveiling at the cemetery with our immediate family. It would not be religious. It would not be formal. It would be just what we wanted it to be...a day for our family to be together and remember Tanner.

Rainbow Around The Son

June 2014

The N-of-1 study was in full swing. Our schedule with Casey consisted of monthly blood draws, when the mobile phlebotomist would come to our house and take her blood. Casey also kept food journals so our team would know what food she was consuming, and this information would be correlated to the results of her monthly draws.

Nik, Laura and Vicki were constantly thinking outside the box and finding new assays that could further our research. Metabolon Labs, in North Carolina, got involved with our project and started studying the metabolites in Casey's blood.

To understand our family's health history, the team had us all do whole-genome sequencing at Illumina in San Diego, California. Whole-genome sequencing is a comprehensive method for analyzing entire genomes. Genomic information is instrumental in identifying inherited disorders, characterizing the mutations that drive cancer progression, and tracking disease outbreak.

In addition to monitoring, imaging and blood, monitoring of microbiome was also very important to the study. Microbiome can be defined as the collection of microbes or microorganisms that inhabit an environment. Researchers have found that microbiome can monitor disease progression. Taking our "above and beyond" approach, our team collected stool samples from Casey to test the microbiome for disease.

Using blood tests, genomics, metabolomics, proteomics and microbiome, we would learn as much as we could about Casey's health.

6.8.14

We headed down to La Jolla to shoot more footage for our movie. We had already filmed at my home and at the cemetery. Now it was the scientific stuff...the medical component.

6.10.14

It was an incredible day of filming at the J. Craig Venter Institute. Casey was also a part of the movie and did a great job. We shot footage in the lab, and I interviewed the doctors on our team. We talked about the Tanner Project, what it entails, its enormous importance and its goals.

My interview with Dr. Venter...wow...it was amazing. It was such a great honor to be in the position to interview such a revered and famous scientist.

As the sun set, we headed back home. I felt so good about the day of filming at JCVI. I couldn't wait to see it all incorporated in our Tanner Project movie.

6.15.14

I had a phone call with Vicki. You know, it's so interesting what our blood says about us. Now that we are analyzing the metabolites in Casey's blood, we see things that one would not normally see in a standard blood test.

When Casey had her blood drawn back in April, they found an artificial sweetener in her system. Thinking back to the days before her blood was drawn, we had been in Palm Desert and Casey had indulged in various sweet drinks that most likely contained artificial sweeteners. Amazingly, just a few drinks showed a high amount in her system. This is just one example of how precise these tests are.

July 2014

I headed down to La Jolla and the CG Creative offices for a day of helping with edits on our movie. It would be an emotional day...but I was excited. It was all coming together.

When we started this, I didn't know what to expect. We had a few bumps in the road but, in the end, the footage turned out beautifully.

I sat on a couch in the editing bay and watched as the screens above me projected the film footage. It was so important that everything turn out perfectly. Every shot, every beat, every edit... it all had to flow, to feel right...to be perfect.

There was a scene where we used home-movie footage of Tanner singing. I was narrating; at the end I say the words, "He never lost his smile," and at the same time as I say those words, the video shows Tanner smiling. I knew the exact beat I wanted...how my narration should flow over the video. I knew how I wanted every scene to be edited, and so I gave instructions, sharing with the editor exactly how I thought it should be. It was great...I was in my element.

7.24.14

I had another Tanner dream.

My phone rang and it read "Eloise" on the caller ID. I answered it. It was Tanner. "Mommy!" he cried. Tanner was trying to talk to me. He kept saying something, but I couldn't understand him. I thought he was saying something with the word "Adam" in it. I would repeat what I thought I had heard, and he became frustrated with me, saying "No, Mommy." Then he would repeat it again. He did this several times, but I couldn't make out his words over the static and noise. I just couldn't understand him. He finally said, "Forget it Mommy. I'll tell you later." But I knew there was no "later." I said, "Tanner, wait!" I told him how much I loved him. How he was my number one guy and I loved him more than anything in the world. I said to him, "Tanner, I am so proud of you." And he said, "Bye Mommy."

Shit...that dream felt so real.

August 2014

What we have gone through...it is enough to last a lifetime. You don't realize how strong you are, until you go through something like this. You don't realize your capabilities, until you have to be there...thrust into the situation with no choice.

The last thing I wanted to deal with, after Tanner's illness and death, was having to go into a hospital again. Having to deal with a child of mine having an MRI, a blood test, an appointment with an oncologist. But I had no choice. To keep Casey healthy, I had to deal with all of this and more.

Casey is truly the most amazing girl. I'm not just a Mom bragging about her daughter... she truly is. The shit she has had to deal with when she could have rebelled. But she didn't. It empowered her. It made her stronger.

Earlier in the year, Casey had heard about a program at Children's Hospital Los Angeles. It's called Camp CHLA. For one week, participants shadow different department specialists at the hospital. It is a competitive selection process, and Casey was one of a few incoming sophomores accepted into the program.

The one thing that made Camp CHLA easier for me...and for her...was that CHLA didn't have any significant ties to Tanner's illness. This was not a "sick place hospital" for Tanner. Except for our meeting with Dr. Finlay, who originally told us about the p53 gene, Tanner hadn't gone to CHLA. He didn't go to clinic there. He didn't have treatment there. This was a "safe" place for our family, because it wasn't associated with Tanner.

8.8.14

I was so very proud. Today Casey completed the week-long program at Children's Hospital Los Angeles. One of sixty-nine high school kids that were accepted into Camp CHLA, Casey shadowed specialists in fields like radiation oncology, nursing, child life, social work and genetic counseling. She spent a lot of time on the oncology floor...not easy, as one can imagine. The sick kids reminded her of Tanner, and the journey that we experienced. How hard it must have been, yet she took the high road and got the most out of every moment there...making friends, sharing her story and learning every day. Who knows where this may take her? Wherever that may be, she will always remember this incredible experience. What a way to end the summer.

Casey started school...tenth grade. Time goes so fast...yet stands still.

8.13.14

I didn't know what propelled my crazy urge to do some deep cleaning. Maybe it was the end of summer, and Casey back at school. But it was time to really discard stuff. Little did I know what a trip down memory lane it would be, going through boxes and boxes. Reading letters, looking at pictures...it helped a lot. It brought me back to a time when "all was okay." Even before that...it brought me back to a time, when I wasn't someone's wife or mom...I was Marlo.

I was still not ready to go through Tanner's stuff. So I kept the door to his room closed, only going in once in a while to breathe it all in. I also had a lot of his stuff downstairs in our family room. I wasn't really ready to deal with that either, but Casey needed a room where she could hang out with her friends (somewhere beside her bedroom), so the family room needed to be cleaned.

I decided to start with organizing the boxes in the garage to make room for Tanner's belongings. I didn't know what I would find. I knew there would be a lot of Tanner in there, and I wasn't sure, if I was ready to open those boxes of memories. Instead, I focused on the old stuff. The really old stuff. And I'm glad I did.

Marlo Gottfurcht Longstreet

I have always been the kind of person who saved stuff. I always thought that my kids would want to see what I have collected and saved from my past, including my years in camp and school. So, for the past few days, in between conference calls, I have been opening boxes and, for the first time in a long time, I've smiled a lot.

As I opened these boxes, the memories all came flooding back. We didn't have computers. We didn't have Internet. We wrote notes every day and we would pass these notes to each other in class. We would write notes at home (when we should have been doing our homework) and give them to each other the next day in school. I have so many notes from Kim (who always signed them "Kim K." - as if I didn't know who she was), from Shani, from Jill, Nicole, Allison, Lainie, Joanna, Dayna, Debbie, Louis, Deb, Dina, Magen, Jen and Lisa. My elementary and middle school years at El Rodeo. My high school years at Beverly. The summer of camp at French Woods. College years at Loyola Marymount University. I have love notes (those are the best)...from my eighth grade boyfriend (you know who you are), my camp boyfriends (I would love to know where they are today), my high school boyfriend (no comment) and of course, tons from Greg.

I have so many pictures. Pictures that made me remember how simple life was, although it hadn't seemed that way at the time. Pictures from pool parties, from Bar/Bat mitzvahs, from camp, from my Sweet Sixteen, from prom and sorority parties. I looked at those pictures and wondered how and why things turned out the way they did.

I found an essay I had written in 1981...fifth grade. The topic was where I would be in 2001. Ironically that's the year Tanner was born. In 1981, I wrote that in 2001 I thought I would be married to Elan S. (I'm sure I wasn't the only girl who thought that) and living in Brentwood or Beverly Hills. I would be either a real estate developer or an actress, and I would have two kids...a girl and then three years later a boy (well, that part came true.) Things were just so simple then.

I miss those days. If I knew then what I know now...sigh. I wish I could go back and have a conversation with teenage Marlo. Tell her what I know. I would whisper in her ear and tell her the secrets that would change her life, and how very different life might have been.

But I have no regrets. I married a great guy, and we remained good friends even after our divorce. And I had the two greatest children I could ask for. My life has been marked with tragedy, and I wish things could have been different. But it is what it is. So I move forward, looking at notes, looking at pictures, and remembering back to a time when life was so innocent and carefree.

September 2014

After all these months of work, the Tanner Project movie was officially complete. I was so proud of the final product. It realistically presented our journey, our lives and plans for the Tanner Project, which we hoped would save lives in the future.

We drove down to La Jolla to show the final cut to Dr. Venter and his team.

9.12.14

HOLY SHIT!!!!! OH MY GOD!!! I was stunned. I just could not believe what happened today. Truly...I am still without words. Humbled and honored.

We showed the finished movie to Dr. Venter, his wife (and publicist) Heather, and a few others. Fourteen minutes later, he told us he loved it. They all loved it. And then Dr. Venter asked me something I would never forget: to present the movie and speak at the JCVI black tie gala the following month.

I was speechless. I was flattered. I was honored. When I look in the mirror I see this Mom, who still drives a minivan, gets juice boxes from the market and cleans up goldfish cracker crumbs. But I am a Mom whose life changed in an instant. I am a Mom with a huge purpose, and I know I have an important message that needs to be shared. I am so thankful to Dr. Venter for giving me this incredible opportunity. I can…I will…make an impact on everyone, and this was just the beginning.

9.26.14

I am so excited! The Tanner Project Foundation logo was finally complete…and it is just perfect. A few months after Tanner died, when we decided to start a Foundation, as a favor to me, Claudio worked on some logos for us. He travels the world and is always on an airplane, so maybe he came up with the beginning of what would become our amazing logo, while he was cruising at 30,000 feet!

It was a combination of an image of Tanner, our Foundation name and our motto: Reach for Hope. After some fine-tuning, back and forth changes and color adjustments, our logo was born.

October 2014

It was the beginning of our weekend in La Jolla. A weekend of meetings, the JCVI Black Tie Gala and a great dinner with the CG Creative crew.

10.18.14

What a beautiful night. Perfect weather. Stars in the sky. I will always remember this night...how proud I was to be a guest speaker at the J. Craig Venter Institute's Annual Black Tie Gala in La Jolla. So amazed. So honored and so humbled. Another moment to go down, as a night I will never forget.

Nik introduced me, and I carefully climbed the stairs to the stage. The 200 plus guests had just watched our Tanner Project movie, and the spotlight was now on me. I took a deep breath and read my speech:

I am Casey and Tanner's Mom. I am Marlo.

Marlo Gottfurcht Longstreet

I had the perfect life. My kids were great. I was great (yes, I was divorced, but even that was great, since I was, and still am, very good friends with my ex-husband). I lived the perfect life. But then something happened that changed my world, my everything, and nothing was ever the same again. It sounds so clichéd, but it is true. You think it can never happen to you to your family. But it does happen. It did happen. And, yes we will never be the same again.

Today is seventeen months since my son Tanner passed away. And in this moment, I can't think of a more appropriate place for me to be, right here, right now, than sharing my story with you tonight.

When Tanner was first diagnosed with a glioblastoma, we, like any other diligent parents, went and got a second opinion, and then a third and then a fourth. One of the doctors we met was Dr. Jonathan Finlay, a pediatric neuro-oncologist who was then at Children's Hospital Los Angeles. It was Dr. Finlay who sat us down and right away asked us the most important question...what is your family history? At the time, there was no cancer in my family. But my ex-husband Greg had it in his. His mom had breast cancer in her early thirties and passed away at forty-nine.

It was at Dr. Finlay's suggestion that we had Tanner tested for the mutant p53 gene. A month later we found out Tanner was positive. Greg and I were next to be tested. I am negative. Greg is the carrier.

And as you just watched in our movie, our daughter Casey is also positive for the mutant p53 gene. The rest is history.

At Tanner's funeral I spoke and tonight, I want to share with you one of the things I said:

Tanner had a higher purpose...and now it is my purpose...my goal...to keep his memory alive. To have his legacy live on. It is now my mission to take our tragedy and turn it around. Because of Tanner, others will live. Because of him, others will have a chance. Because of him, our world will be a different place, a better place. Tanner is our hero.

Soon after Tanner passed away, with my dad by my side, we began our journey and created the Tanner Project Foundation. We traveled. We spoke to different doctors. Visited different institutions. We asked questions. We listened. We became frustrated. No one would help us go above and beyond to keep Casey healthy. We needed to make sure this didn't happen again to us...to our family...or to anyone else.

In January, 2014, less than a year ago, my dad and I walked into this building and met with Dr. Nicholas Schork. The building had just opened, and we drove past it a couple of times...there was no name on the building. And we just couldn't believe this beautiful structure could be a lab! We met with Nik, and told him our story. I shared a conversation I had had with Casey the week before. We were driving to get her yearly scans done and she asked me, "Mommy I'm getting my scans today and they may show I'm ok, but what about tomorrow? What if cancer happens tomorrow? Do we have to wait a whole year for scans to see the cancer?" I looked at Casey and didn't know what to say...she was right. What about tomorrow? It was in that moment, I knew the protocol had to change.

We asked Nik if there were a way we could monitor Casey every day, 24/7, to make sure she stays healthy. Nik told us that's called an N-of-1 study, and that was what he wanted to do...N-of-1 studies at JCVI. Nik explained that what they would learn from Casey would help others...N-of-1 for everyone.

It was thirteen years ago that Dr. Craig Venter sequenced his own genome, and THAT was an N-of-1 study for everyone. At that moment, I felt like Tanner led us to Nik. To JCVI. It was perfect timing. The Tanner Project was born.

Since then, we have met the most brilliant, incredible, kind, warm and supportive people. Our director, Dr. Nicholas Schork, Dr. Craig Venter, Dr. Karen Nelson, Dr. Laura Goetz, Heather Kowalski and all of the researchers and scientists who work daily on the Tanner Project...because of all of you, Casey has a chance...and others will have a chance.

A special thank you to Nik and Laura for all of your dedication... every day...you have gone above and beyond and we will forever *be grateful. Thank you for listening to us. Thank you for taking us under your wing...a father and a daughter with a mission in life.*

Casey couldn't be here tonight, because she is on a school trip to Washington DC. She lives a normal life. She is turning sixteen in a month. She dances competitively with her dance team. She is a great student, a great friend, a great daughter. She is proud to be a part of this study. She knows it keeps her healthy, and she knows that by doing her part she will be helping others.

In the beginning, Casey was private about her mutant gene, but she has recently decided to start spreading the word. This diagnosis and project has empowered her. She, too, wants to make a difference. She's not going to let the fact that she has an over 90% chance of getting cancer get in the way of living. She lives life to the fullest every single day. Happy. Joyous. And full of love and laughter. What more could a mother want for her daughter?

As for her brother, we talk about Tanner all the time. We miss him more than words can say.

As for me...I could be the kind of person who hides under the covers and doesn't want to come out (trust me, there are some days I feel that way). But that's not who I am. I have an incredible daughter who looks at me daily for strength, love and laughter. I do this for her. I do this for the memory of Tanner. I do this because it is what I'm meant to do.

Tanner was eleven and a half years old when he died, but it seemed like he lived a lifetime. As a parent who loses a child, you search. You ask all the questions...the why's, the what's, the how's, and rarely do you get an answer. Tanner was a magical child who is giving us answers. He died so we could take the lessons he taught us and change the world.

Every day I wake up and miss my baby boy. But every day I wake up and know what my purpose is. I know Tanner had a purpose, and his death had meaning. To save lives. To find an answer. Because of the research being done here at JCVI...because of our N-of-1 study, I believe the pieces of the puzzle will fit together.

To know my son's name is associated with a project that is being talked about, that is revered, that is one-of-a-kind and innovative. To know that all of you here tonight say "Tanner Project" and that's my son...that's Tanner. I couldn't be more proud.

My family...we had the perfect life. It changed in a heartbeat. It happened to me...to my family...to us. It could happen to anyone. It could happen to you. Let's make sure it doesn't.

10.31.14

Halloween...our second one without him.

I still bought large size candy bars to hand out. I still called it Tanner's Candy Store. I still imagined him on the couch, iPad in hand, watching my every move.

November begins tomorrow.

November 2014

I was still relishing the excitement of my speaking at the Gala. That is something that doesn't go away. I was glad I had something to make me smile as we headed into this month...the birthday month.

This month was harder than usual. Casey turned sixteen. Sweet Sixteen. How happy Tanner would have been for her! How excited he would have been to drive with her, after she got her driver's license. "Bye Mom, we're going out," he would have yelled to me. My two babies in the front seat...oh how I wish he were here.

It was important to me for Casey to have the perfect Sweet Sixteen party. Her favorite meal was brunch, so that's what we did. We hosted a beautiful brunch for her friends, both guys and girls, at a hotel close to home. Photo booth, music, flash tattoos... we did it all and it was perfect.

Marlo Gottfurcht Longstreet

11.25.14

A Letter To My Son On His Thirteenth Birthday

Dear Tanner,

Today you would have been thirteen. Wow...that's hard to say out loud..."would have been"...that past tense just sucks. Even after a year and a half, I'm still not used to it.

Today you would have woken up in my bed...because that's where you slept. But actually, now that you were thirteen, those days would have been behind us, and you would have been in your own bed. I would have given you tons of kisses and cuddles and looked at you, with a big smile and said, "Happy Birthday Tanner... you're a teenager!" And you would have smiled back.

You would have gone downstairs to see cards and presents and balloon decorations to celebrate your special day. Maybe you would have wanted Daddy to come over and make you pancakes, or maybe you simply would have wanted an apple juice and banana for your birthday breakfast.

We would have made the day about you. Whatever you wanted to do, we would have done. No "mommy errands" - just stuff for Tanner. Maybe we would have gone miniature golfing. Maybe it would have been a trip to Walmart. Or to the pier. Or maybe you would have wanted to stay home all day and watch

SpongeBob and order LA Bites. Maybe you would have had a Bar Mitzvah that we would have celebrated last weekend. All of this we will never know.

I would have told you how proud I was of you. What a big boy you had become. I would have told you how amazing it was to be your Mom. I would have told you to blow out the candles on your cake, to make a wish and for all of your wishes to come true. You probably would have gone out with Casey…now that she is driving…wow…that would have been something you would have loved. Driving off with Casey and doing your thing.

Today I would have had you light the candle that burns down each year as we celebrate each birthday. The candle that goes to the age of sixteen, and that Casey just lit last week.

We would have had your birthday dinner at Lawry's. You would have ordered no salad, but definitely prime rib, mashed potatoes and "peas please" (and yes, of course, no gravy or au jus on the plate). You would have eaten every single bite. You would have ordered the warm chocolate cake for dessert, and you would have wanted it all to yourself. You would have had a good day. Thirteen would have been good.

But a parent's worst nightmare has happened. You are no longer here with me…with us. Time has passed, but honestly, it isn't any easier. We go about our days. We work. We play. We try our best. But in the end...at the end of the day...our hearts are empty. There is a piece missing that will never, ever be replaced.

So today, on what would have been your thirteenth, Tanner, I celebrate you. We all celebrate you. My baby boy who would have been a teenager...the most loving, sweetest, cuddly, mushy, funny, special boy who was the bravest kid I have ever known. Thank you for being in our lives...even for so brief of a time. Thank you for giving us so much love and laughter.

December 2014

Another year has gone by. Birthdays, holidays, the New Year. Every day is a new day without Tanner. Does it get easier? No, it doesn't.

I always have loved seeing the holiday lights this time of year. The different colors. The festive feel. The smell of the Christmas tree. The buying and wrapping of presents. Except now, it just was not the same.

January 2015

Another New Year.

People tell me how they love what I write on Facebook. I don't plan it or schedule my remarks. I don't bombard people with my feelings…I just write when the mood strikes. I don't really find the words…the words find me.

And then, when I'm ready to write, I write.

1.4.15

Today I turned forty-four.

Last night, Casey and I fell asleep a little after midnight, with her wishing me a happy birthday, and me with tears streaming down my face. I wished that there were some rule that, at least on your birthday, those who are no longer here could magically appear to give you some birthday love. I woke up this morning with Casey asleep by my side. The sun was shining, the sky was blue, and it was the sounds of texts, from those that I love so much, that made me smile.

Casey gave me my birthday gift...the most incredible gift from a daughter to a mother. She wrote me the most beautiful letter, full of love and admiration. She explained in her letter what her present to me would be. She wrote: *"I know what we've been through is terrible, and no one should ever have to experience what our family went through. You lost one of your babies; it's the worst thing that could happen. I know nothing can replace him or make it better, but I want you to know how much you are loved. Not only by your family and friends, but my friends as well. I asked my closest friends whom you know to write a birthday message for you, and the results I got are absolutely beautiful. Most of my friends think of you as a second mom and are extremely grateful to have you in their lives. Nothing can ever replace Tanner, but I want you to know you have all of this powerful love, from actual kids and not just the adults you are surrounded by. You are just so loved."*

Just take a moment to digest this...what Casey did for me. She collected and put together birthday messages...messages of love... from her wonderful friends. With tears in my eyes, I read each and every one. I was speechless...absolutely speechless.

I received so many Facebook Happy Birthday wishes and I wanted to say thank you:

Rainbow Around The Son

If you put your birthday on Facebook, you're expected to get tons of birthday wishes. But even when expected, it's a very humbling experience to read all of the kind wishes from so many special friends. Friends from far and near, friends from childhood, as well as recent friends...they have all put a smile on my face today. Thank you for all of the continued love, support and... today's birthday wishes. How appreciated it all is.

And now...a few words from my heart to yours.

The other day as I was walking through my courtyard, I noticed our lemon tree. It's a nice size tree sitting in a pot. It was given to us by a friend of Greg's the week Tanner died. Back then, it was small and with no fruit. But now it is bigger and fuller, and there were six lemons on its branches. Time had passed. The lemons had appeared.

I was able to get away for a few days. It helps, but it doesn't do the trick. Know what I mean? You may be able to step out of your element to escape, but it is only temporary. Reality follows you wherever you go, but you make the best and most of it... and so I did.

Michael and I went back to Big Sur. Days and nights filled with hiking, yoga, workouts, massages, infinity hot tubs at sunset, deer at the doorstep, good wine, good food, whale watching, collecting rocks and pine cones, frost on the ground, fires in our tree house, walking barefoot across the freezing Big Sur River, Dave Matthews Band playing driving in a convertible and deep breaths of cold, fresh, clean air. A great distraction.

But when it's time to go home, you make that long trek down the mountain. You look to your right. You see the big, blue, vast beautiful ocean and reality comes rushing back. You think about the year ending...the New Year approaching. You think about what you have done this year, and what you want to do next. You think about your friends, your family, the ones you love, really love, the most. You think about what you can change...what you can do to make a difference. You think about the ones you miss so very much. You think about it all.

We ring in the New Year by counting down. I had fourteen teenagers at my home, counting down, celebrating the New Year and never sleeping. A home full of kids, smiles, laughter, happiness, friendship...the perfect way for Casey to say happy New Year. For me, the Mom, it's a little harder. So bittersweet...seeing your daughter so happy, but feeling the absence of the little boy who should be there, too.

Last New Year, 2013 going into 2014, I was so sad that the year was starting without Tanner here to experience it, to be a part of it. We were entering a year that Tanner would never live to see. Instead of saying, "Tanner died this year" I would have to say "Tanner died last year." Now...in 2015, it's even worse. It will be two years. Two years! It seems unimaginable. That's the hardest part of a new year, marking the vast distance between one year and the next, when everything changed.

So, in this year, 2015, I will continue to put one foot in front of the other. I will watch Casey grow and continue to be the most brave, incredible young woman I know. I will continue my dedication and hard work on the Tanner Project...preaching "Knowledge is Power" over and over again. I will try and go out a little more (I do miss my girlfriends).

In 2015, I hope to do more, see more, learn more. I hope to have continued good health...amazing love...and yes, more smiles and laughter.

1.14.15

People often ask me how I am doing. I'm just okay. But I'm trying...trying to allow myself some moments of goodness.

Yesterday, as I was leaving a meeting and getting into an elevator to go down to the parking area, someone asked me what floor I was going to and, repeating one of Tanner's favorite lines, I said "P2 and yes, I do need to pee too." Everyone laughed. Tanner would have been proud that his Mommy made a funny in an elevator.

Work continued and kept me busy. I had been asked to speak at another event, Abundance 360, on behalf of Human Longevity, Inc., Dr. Venter's other venture. I would show my movie and speak to a room of 300. It could be 3 or 300 or 3,000...it made no difference to me. I would look out at the sea of faces and say what I needed to say...share what I needed to share. This was my journey. This is what I was supposed to do. Tanner's death had meaning...and it was now my job and purpose to articulate that meaning to help others...to save others.

This week would be filled with hope. With experience. With tears. With smiles. With success. With opportunity. With awesomeness. With sharing our story. This week would be filled with amazing moments...more moments of goodness.

February 2015

I still struggled. I struggled with my daily life, my friendships, my relationship. I struggled with the good and the bad. I struggled with what I had and what I really wanted.

2.2.15

I met a friend for lunch today and she said something so profound that I wrote it down on a post-it and kept it in my car:

> I'd rather be sitting in traffic
> than be sitting in a hospital.

2.7.15

I have been remembering certain things that happened before Tanner got sick, things that could possibly have made our journey very different.

About five or six years ago, after Greg and I separated, I remembered having a tough day with Tanner. I don't remember the details, but I was frustrated, exhausted, about to give up. I needed a break. A time out for Mommy. I went up to my room and locked the door. I just needed a few minutes to myself. To breathe. To collect my thoughts. I called my dad to vent.

Suddenly, I saw Tanner on the roof, peering into my window. "Hi, Mommy," he causally said, with a smile on his face. I screamed and hung up the phone. My window was open, but it had a screen on it. I punched out the screen and told Tanner to slowly come towards me. I pulled him into safety. I was so mad, yet relieved that he was safe.

I was dumbfounded. How the hell did he get up on the roof? I went downstairs and saw that the front door that leads into our courtyard was open...and there was his concoction. He had used a chair, some books and a step stool and, balancing atop it all, he had hoisted himself up to the roof.

Another time, in January 2011, Tanner was playing in his room. I peeked in. He was sitting on the floor with all his toys. I walked downstairs and put my shoes on...we were going out to run some errands. Casey and I were ready. I called to Tanner from the bottom of the stairs and told him we had to go. He walked to the top of the stairs, looked at me...and fell over. He had lost consciousness. I bolted up the stairs and caught him about three quarters of the way down. He had hit his head. He was blue and not moving. I noticed a toy had wrapped itself around his neck. When I pulled it off, he started to scream. I knew he would be okay, but we nevertheless called 911, and an ambulance arrived. Two hours later, after a CAT scan and a doctor's assurance that he was fine, we went home.

Those times come back to me: the roof episode, falling down the stairs. He could have died each time, but he didn't. Had he died on one of those occasions, it would have been a tragedy. An accident. We never would have known about the p53, his mutant gene, until it might have been too late for Greg or Casey or both. It was because of his brain tumor that we knew. And were able to save his dad and his sister.

Greg's mom developed breast cancer in her early thirties and died at forty-nine. I actually met her the night before she died. Greg and I had just started to date. For years, when I would have my mammogram, I would ask the radiologist about Greg's mom and how her illness could impact Casey (I never even thought about asking how it could impact Tanner...or Greg). At first, and this is going back over ten years ago, the radiologist told me that if the breast cancer had occurred on the father's side of the family, Casey didn't need to worry as much. I think the thought back then was it "counted more," if there was a history of cancer on the mother's side. Such bullshit. Then later on, through the years, I was merely told Casey should probably get mammograms at thirty-five instead of forty. I really thought there was nothing to worry about. I, myself, was getting mammograms in my early thirties, because a close friend of mine was diagnosed with breast cancer in her early thirties. I refused to wait until forty, even with no family history.

There is another lesson in this. An important lesson that is often ignored or not understood. Yes, women can pass on their cancer genes...*but so can men.* Many people think you can only get a breast cancer gene from your mother, from a female. This is not true. Dads can also pass on the BRCA gene, as well as the p53 gene (as Greg did) and many other cancer genes, to both female and male children. Many individuals have a hereditary cancer gene which was passed on from their father (and not their mother). Look no further than my own children to see the proof.

I have learned, through all of this, the importance of being proactive. The importance of speaking up...having your voice heard. I always speak my mind. Doctors' medical opinions are not gospel. If something is not right...if you want a treatment or test that they are not recommending, insist on it. It is so important to think outside the box.

Years ago, when Tanner was six or seven, we decided to see a genetic counselor about his developmental delays. It was important to have this information for the future, when both

Casey and Tanner had their own kids. If there was a genetic issue, they should be aware of it, before they started their own families.

The genetic counselor we contacted was known to be the top in the field. We filled out form after form. We were interviewed. Tanner had a genetic blood test. Everything came back normal. They told us we could take the next step and do more extensive testing for Tanner. We decided to do it and all still seemed to be fine. There were no issues or genetic problems. No genetic connection to Tanner's delays, processing and speech issues.

But guess what? Guess what they didn't notice? Yup...cancer. Disease. I am certain that somewhere in the many forms we filled out, there would have been a question about Tanner's grandparents. We would have noted Greg's mom developed cancer at a young age and had passed away.

This is one example when thinking outside the box is so important. Yes, we were there to search for answers for Tanner's development delays - but, and this is a big "but," - there was more that should have been asked and answered. How about a genetic counselor looking at our forms and observing: "I know you're here for Tanner's developmental delays, but I see there's cancer, at a young age, in your family history. It's only one cancer, but it was breast cancer at a young age, and that is a red flag. You may want to consider testing for more." Did anyone consider this line of inquiry? No. And I didn't have the knowledge or information to ask more questions. Today I do.

Genetic testing…growth hormones. Different areas, but the same bottom line. No one thought outside the box.

Had we known any of this…our outcome might have been so different.

Knowledge is Power.

2.20.15

Since Tanner's death, I have tried very hard not to think back to his last moments. I am very open about everything that happened, but when it comes to remembering the last few breaths he took, I just can't go there. Watching his chest rise and fall, rise and fall…and then stop. Ugh…it's way too painful…way too hard. So when those terrible memories come crashing through, I have learned to shake them out of my head. Literally, physically, I shake my head to get rid of the "noise." That's what I call those bad memories…"noise." I just don't want to remember.

March 2015

I am a believer – in dreams with meanings, in coincidences with deeper connotations, in the symbolism of inexplicable moments, like the rainbow around the sun.

Since Tanner died, things have happened that made me think twice.

When you lose someone close to you, you look at the world with different eyes. Whether it is noticing every butterfly that flutters by, or looking at a bunch of weeds and seeing a single flower in bloom, or trying to make sense of the fact that the lights are flickering in your home...when you see things through different eyes, they take on new meanings.

There were some things, though, that really made me wonder. The night Tanner died, our first night without him, I went into my room to close the windows. It was 12:30 a.m. on May 19. I heard a bird chirping. Then another bird. It was a shrill chirp, yet during all the nights I had been with Tanner, I had never heard a bird singing or chirping at night.

The day after Tanner died, I was trying to print something on my printer, but the machine wouldn't work. When the pages finally began to come out of the printer, two odd ones appeared. One had weird lines all over it. The other had gibberish nonsense symbols. That had never happened before.

Both Casey and Tanner were born to Beck songs. At Tanner's funeral, Greg made a play list of songs that were important to our family, which played while the guests arrived. Right before the service, Greg went in to see Tanner in his coffin (I didn't go. I just couldn't). A Beck song was playing as Greg said his final goodbye.

The rainbow around the sun at Tanner's funeral…no explanation for that. My love ring being lost then found? And the picture of Tanner and the Tesla from the Vanilla Bake Shop window? Truly no words.

The day after Tanner's funeral, the songs I heard on the radio were: "Knocking on Heaven's Door," "Heaven," "Locked out of Heaven" and "Die Young."

The night after Tanner's funeral, Casey asked to cuddle with me. The way she wrapped herself around me was exactly the way Tanner and I had cuddled: his feet next to mine, his chest resting against my head, my hand on his hip. It was him. I felt him. The nights before and the nights after Tanner died, she had cuddled with me the way she always had. This night was different.

In fact, as I sit here and remember these moments, a bird with a red breast (Tanner's favorite color) comes hopping into my office. Never before has this happened. Hello Tanner!

Ten days after Tanner died, on my way to visit my mom at the hospital, I walked around the block to my favorite restaurant, The Ivy. I had called in advance to get a gift certificate for a friend. I was told it would be waiting for me at the hostess stand. A waiter tried to help me, but couldn't find it, so he left me waiting for a few minutes. I looked down at the hostess desk, and on a note pad in blue highlighter, was written the name "Tanner." The waiter came back and realized the card had been sitting at the desk the whole time. Had he given it to me right away, I wouldn't have seen the word "Tanner" written down on that pad.

One night, I was on my couch with Michael. We had the front door open to let the breeze in. I was talking to Michael when something caught my eye at the door. It was Tanner. More clear than ever. Tanner held the door frame with his right hand and sauntered in. He was wearing his UGG boots and pajamas, as he usually would wear. I started to breath very fast. I couldn't control it. I felt like I was hyperventilating. The tears just flowed...I couldn't stop. And in the next moment, it was over. Tanner was gone.

You might think that, in some cases, I was overreaching, looking for things that weren't there. Trying to find meaning in even the simplest things. But, at the end of the day, I gotta do what I gotta do...whatever makes my heart feel just a little better.

3.10.15

Casey's leg has been hurting. We think it is because of dancing, a muscle injury, perhaps. But it scared me. I didn't want to worry and jump to conclusions about every ache and pain, but how could I not? I live in that kind of world now. Jumping to conclusions, knowing bad things can happen...that kind of world.

3.14.15

We went to the doctor yesterday to check Casey's leg. The doctor thought it was simply a hip flexor sprain, and that rest would help. But "rest" is not in the vocabulary of a dancer who was in the middle of competition season.

Casey has her bi-annual MRI in a few weeks, and I will make sure the MRI focuses on her affected leg. Just to be safe. I emailed one of her doctors and told her what was going on. She agreed that it's probably her hip flexor...that this makes the most sense.

She also told me that she would check Casey's previous scans to see what the area looked like in the past. I told her it was Casey's left leg that was bothering her.

Several hours later, I remembered writing something down about a year ago, after Casey had had a previous scan. I searched for the note and found it. It was about something that was found on her left femur, something benign. I had been told not to worry, that this was a common occurrence in teenagers. I took a deep breath. Left femur. Fuck...this new pain was also in the left leg. A different part of the leg, but still, it was the same leg. I emailed the doctor and asked about it...really trying not to jump to any conclusions.

The doctor responded the next day. The area from last year, which is near the knee, is commonly seen in teenagers and generally benign. I shouldn't worry. The place Casey was now complaining about is higher up and not in a "cancer place." I would still make sure that the MRI would focus on that area. But for now, I am relieved.

Today, she didn't even have pain.

3.17.15

Tomorrow will mark twenty-two months since Tanner left us. In two months it will be two years. That seems like such a long time.

I went to the cemetery today. I do that about once a week. Sometimes it stretches to eight, nine, ten days. I never stay away more than two weeks.

So, today I went and brought red roses, as I always do, and I talked to my guy. Sometimes I talk to him in my head…sometimes I say the words aloud. Today, I asked him if he could just come visit me. Just for a minute. Just so I could see him again. I tell him if it's against "the rules" not to worry…it would be our secret…I wouldn't tell anyone. I just want to see him again.

After a while, I left Tanner's grave and headed back to my car. On the way, I checked out Tanner's "neighborhood." I often see new plots that were not there on my last visit. It makes you realize the cycle of life…birth, life, death. Your life can turn in an instant. One of Tanner's newest neighbors is Leonard Nimoy. That made me smile, knowing he was just down the path from my guy.

I was starting to think about the next few years, something I rarely do, since I tend not to plan ahead anymore. Not since Tanner got sick. But I was starting to think about the future. Before I know it, Casey will be off to college. What will I do? Where will I be? Do I move? Start over? Or stay in my home and continue my life as it is now? Who will I be?

As parents, as a Mom, our children define us. I was busy with work and the Foundation, but at 2:15 p.m. every weekday, when Casey came home from school, and even though she drives now, I go into Mom mode. What will happen when she leaves for college? When she becomes an adult? What happens to us? To the Moms and Dads? What happens when there are no kids at home? I was supposed to have Tanner here. Now, I didn't know my place. I was lost.

I think of my future. Where will I feel the happiest? Where will I feel at peace? Is there a place where I can be ME again? Is it here in Los Angeles? Or in Newport Beach? La Jolla? Big Sur? New York? Where do I belong?

3.25.15

It was that time of the year again. Casey's dance competition in Redondo Beach...Hall of Fame. I will always remember it was there that Tanner saw her dance for the last time. Was it really two years ago?

For the past four years, Casey has been dedicated to dance. And, of course, the past few years have been so very hard for us. But it was dancing that became Casey's constant...her therapy and escape.

She had worked so hard, and it showed.

As we drove down to the competition on Thursday night, tears rolled down Casey's face. How sad she was. She took all of that...her emotions about Tanner, her sadness, her anger, her frustration, her passion, her dedication, her love and put it into her performances that weekend. And, boy did it show.

Casey's solo performance won a platinum and sixth overall. Casey's duet won a first place platinum and first overall. Casey was also invited to perform in an opening number at Nationals in Las Vegas. Casey's Senior Team group pieces were also fantastic. We were so proud.

3.29.15

Tonight I watched "60 Minutes." But, I was not prepared for the emotions that hit me tonight.

The program described how Duke University was treating glioblastomas (GBM) by injecting the polio virus into the tumor. How incredible that was. I watched this episode and the tears wouldn't stop. GBM is a death sentence. Most people don't survive a GBM. Their lives might be prolonged a little with extensive surgery, chemotherapy and radiation, but GBM is a bad, bad disease. To watch this show and see people being told their GBM is gone, well...I have no words.

3.30.15

I've done some soul searching lately. It is helpful to do that every now and then. I haven't seen many of my friends. I haven't gone out a lot. I've been working hard...Tanner Project work... and some other little projects that I was tackling with my heart and soul. I have also been taking care of myself and trying to learn to be a little more selfish. It is good to do that, too, every now and then.

Casey was more independent...yes, she still needed me...but I was realizing that I could do more...for myself. I was proud of that. It has taken me a long time to get here. I was still mourning. I was sad. I didn't smile as much as I used to and I don't laugh like I once did. But I wanted to do more. Share more. I knew good things were on the horizon for me, and I was ready for them.

April 2015

I still sleep in the same bed that Tanner died in. The same side. The same spot. The same old mattress. I'm not ready to give it up for a new one quite yet (although my back would tell you different). Every night, as I get into bed, I think about this... that this is where he died. I know it would probably be easier if I got a new mattress...I'm just not ready yet.

4.20.15

Tanner and I had this "thing" with our eyes. It was an unsaid thing, but the way we looked at each other in our eyes was telling. We got each other. I think I've only had that with one other person, besides Tanner.

I really think it's the eyes that can say so much...sometimes more than words. I can look at a picture of Tanner and see him through his eyes. Yes, it is hard to capture in a picture, because real life is so much more compelling. But I couldn't have real life. I had to settle with what I have.

Before this nightmare began, I used to look at people's eyes to see if the tragedy and sadness they had known were reflected there. It was something about the eyes, in and around, that really showed what people have been through. The Sadness. The Loss. The Love. The Memory. The Remembrance. And, yes, even a glimpse of Happiness. Am I now, one of those people? Can you look at me and see what I have been through…through my eyes? I often looked in the mirror asking myself that exact question. I don't see my sparkle anymore…will I ever have it again?

4.25.15

Casey has decided to go public about her mutant p53 gene and she discussed with us how she wanted to do it. Because of her journey, she knew how important it was for people to know about genetics and genomics. She wanted to share that message with her peers all over the world. She started to work on her initiative. She called it "Genome Generation."

4.27.15

A while ago, I made the decision to write my book…*Rainbow Around The Son*. Several friends suggested I write a book, and it was something I, too, had thought about. After reading some of my journal entries, I knew I had something to share. So I started to compile it all...my private thoughts, my journal entries, my Facebook posts...and put everything down in one place.

Over the weekend, Casey and I were at a dance competition and convention. I knew I would have some down time, so I printed up "my work in progress," put it in a three ring binder and brought it with me.

We were hanging out in our hotel room, and Casey asked if she could read some of the excerpts. I watched her as she carefully read each word. After she finished, she looked at me and said, "Mommy, I don't know who wouldn't want to read this. I lived it every day, and I still want to know what happens." Wow.

Casey then asked me how I was going to end the book. I told her, "There is no ending, it just keeps going, because it's about keeping you healthy." She appreciated what I was saying, but said I still needed an ending. Of course, she was right...I just wasn't sure how to end it. In three weeks, it would be two years since Tanner died. Casey suggested I end the book then...at the two-year anniversary. So, that's what I was going to do.

May 2015

I sit back and cannot believe it has been over a year since ago we met Nik and had our first meeting at JCVI.

Every day our JCVI team is involved in research regarding our N-of-1 project, including outside the box assays, as well as microbiome and other scientific research. We have utilized blood tests from companies like Metabolon, Guardant, Trevigen's Comet Assay and others. We have worked closely, and funded a project, with TGen, a research institute in Phoenix, Arizona. We were intrigued and excited about the research being done with ctDNA (circulating DNA) blood tests...trying to discover whether this test can track the blood of a healthy person, and determine if there are any specks of cancer visible.

Metabolon Labs reported back to us that they found something unusual in Casey's blood...a marker that may be a positive indicator. It was something that they would not typically find in someone with the mutant p53 gene. They need to do more research to see what it all means, but this was a start.

This is exactly what our Tanner Project is about. Why is Casey healthy? What is keeping Casey healthy? Maybe these metabolites that Metabolon have discovered have something to do with why she is healthy? Only time will tell.

5.4.15

May the Fourth Be With You.

Wow…I remember writing that in my journal when Tanner was alive. That's the crazy thing…looking back in time to see what was going on.

I always used to do that. I had a Kate Spade day planner in which I would write down everything I did every day. Now everything is recorded on my phone.

My first memory of writing everything down was in seventh grade. I had this teddy bear calendar, and it was 1983…the year of Bar/Bat Mitzvahs. We had parties every single weekend. One of my best friends, Jill, went into my calendar and wrote down the birthdays of everyone in her family. I think I picked up this habit from Jill, writing things down in order to remember. So, with each new day, I would go back into the calendar and read about what I had been doing on this day the previous year. Maybe this pattern has something to do with how I loved my past. I did love remembering…but only the good stuff.

I was recently sharing this observation with Jill, and laughing about something I remembered she had written in that 1983 calendar. It was her dad's birthday...and he was turning fifty. She referred to him as "Old Man." We were cracking up. To think that we looked at fifty as old. And now, we are slowly but surely approaching that age. Michael is even past fifty. So does that mean I am dating an "old man"?

I still keep my planner on my desk. But it is opened to 2012-2013. I have not refilled the pages to reflect the current year. I keep the pages opened to the time when Tanner was still here.

5.5.15

Someone on Facebook has a child who is sick. Today, she posted about another child with a brain tumor. Pictures of this child came across my feed, and I just broke down. There was something about those pictures that reminded me of Tanner. It was devastating to see what was happening to our children. Our innocent, sweet babies...cancer does not discriminate.

I looked at old pictures today. Pictures that are on an old computer. Pictures of Tanner and Casey, of Greg and me. I look so happy, so bright and glowing. I can see the light and happiness, the sparkle in my eyes. I was smiling. I looked at that person, and I didn't recognize her. I was jealous of her. I wanted to be her...once again. This was six years ago, 2009. How can so much change in so short a time?

I found a video that Tanner made. He was sitting at my computer, and made a funny, really cool video. I don't think I had ever seen it. I love those moments, finding surprises. It made me smile, laugh and cry...all at the same time.

5.10.15

Today was Mother's Day. It was 10:08 a.m. and I had already been to Farmers Market and visited Tanner. Later, we will go visit my mom, who, thankfully, has been feeling better and doing great. Casey and I will spend the afternoon together and then enjoy a special dinner tonight.

I've already been showered with texts and Facebook messages. It is so sweet that so many people thought of me today...an extra special thought.

How did I feel today? Honestly, it sucked. I miss Tanner. So much. He would have been the first one up, and he would have been so excited to give me his card. He loved celebrations like this...ones that honored those he loved so much. He would have made this day so sweet. I craved his warmth, his kisses, his hugs, his little voice. I yearn for all of it.

5.11.15

I know I have to get through the next week. May 18...the day he died. May 21...the day we buried him. Two days that I am dreading so much.

Tonight I am alone. I made dinner. Soup. I worked. I drank a glass of wine. I went into the hot tub. My sciatica is acting up. I sat there in the heat, in the steam and looked up at the stars. A plane cruised overhead. The trees swayed in the wind. I felt the cool breeze on my skin, as the hot water enfolded my body.

I missed the way life used to be. I wanted to take the other road. That fork in the road...I wanted to go left instead of right. I just wanted everything to have been different.

5.13.15

Sheryl Sandberg, the COO of Facebook, recently lost her husband. It was unexpected. She wrote about her loss, remarking that she had become a member of a club no one wants to join. I understood...so very much. I am, for sure, in a club that no one wants to be in.

Sheryl Sandberg posts about her loss on Facebook. She wrote about a conversation she had with a friend about her options. Option A was having her husband. Her friend put his arm around her and said: "Option A is not available. So let's kick the shit out of Option B."

Close to a million people liked her post, and almost half a million commented on it. I was one of them. I simply said: "After losing my eleven-year-old son two years ago, your words ring so true to me. Every day I kick the shit out of Option B...although I so want Option A." It was the truth...I wrote the simple truth. And unbelievably, Sheryl Sandberg responded to my comment. To me! She replied, "I'm so sorry for your loss, Marlo."

Wow.

5.14.15

It rained today. Tanner hated the rain. I love it. I went to the cemetery this morning and planted a few flowers. I am no gardener, and I accidently broke a few of the blooms off their stems. I am not good at this. What I am good at is scattering wood chips. I have discovered that for less than eight dollars, you can buy a huge bag of these chips to sprinkle in the area you are working on, making everything look pretty and clean. I like putting the wood chips around Tanner's grave to freshen it up. So that's what I did. Right before the rain began, I made my son's plot look pretty.

5.15.15

It was Friday. The beginning of the weekend that I dread. That I replay. Days that I remember, but would like to forget. It was at this time, two years ago, that we were in the car driving to Marty's to get Tanner his burgers and fries. It was this time when I filled up my car with gas, and Tanner was too tired to help. It was this time when I got the receipt at the gas station, because he asked me to. "I love receipts," he had said. It was this time that we had driven back home, on the 10 freeway, and I noticed he was falling asleep. It was this time we were stopped at a red light and he said, "We are best friends. We kiss. We cuddle. We sleep in bed together." It was this time when my son was alive.

5.16.15

It was Saturday morning, and I lay quietly in my bed. On this day two years ago, we all surrounded Tanner right in this same bed. In two hours, it would be two years…to the day, not the date. After Tanner died, I count days and dates.

Daisy slept quietly at the foot of the bed. It was cloudy outside. The day Tanner died the sky was blue, and the sun shone brightly.

5.17.15

We went to the cemetery, the three of us...Casey, Greg and me. We talked about decisions we had made after Tanner became ill. Greg told Casey that it was because of my insistence that Tanner not undergo radiation, that he lived a happy last few months.

For me it was a simple decision, one that had been right for our little boy. I knew we had to make every day be a great day; we all knew we would rather have a little less time, as long as Tanner was happy. For Tanner, it was the right decision.

5.18.15

My Facebook Post...

Over the past few days, I have thought a lot about what to write today. In fact, I had it all planned out. But then, unexpected things happened, so I have a little more I want to say.

My friends...you are incredible. From the amazing text I received at sunrise, to coming home to roses and cards, to the many Facebook messages, Instagram comments, voice mails, texts, emails...I have no words. I know time goes on and life goes on, but I so appreciate how you remember and keep Tanner's memory alive. Thank you for making today a little easier.

Rainbow Around The Son

Two years. For us, it's not just about the date…May 18…but the day. This whole weekend has been a weekend of "this time two years ago."

As many of you know, I believe in signs. I believe that when you lose someone close, it's important to keep your mind open and look for the signs. This weekend, on Saturday, I was given a sign.

My Saturday morning was filled with errands. I left the house early and kept thinking that I needed to make sure I kept track of the time…noting when it was a little before 11 a.m. - the time Tanner died.

I've been driving an old family car and when it rains, it rains in the car. I've had it fixed, but the rain still comes in. And when it rains in the car, it messes with the radio. After Thursday night's rain, my radio stopped working. Then, on Saturday morning, the radio began to work again, but only broadcasting one station. I did my marketing and got back in the car. I texted a few friends to pass the time. I was watching the clock, but not in a "this time two years ago" kind of way.

After sitting a while in the Whole Foods parking lot, I was ready to leave. I started the car, and the radio came on to that one working station. The DJ announced a Justin Timberlake song would be coming on next, and then - "SexyBack" comes on. Of course.

"SexyBack" was one of Tanner's favorite songs. When he would call me on my mobile phone, that was his ring tone. It's a song he loved, and he would swing his hips back and forth as he sang along. "SexyBack" was all Tanner...it was his song. I looked at the time...it was 10:45 a.m. It was "that time two years ago." Exactly. I had my sign.

They say it gets easier. That's a load of crap.

In many ways, the second year is harder than the first. That first year sucks beyond belief. The year of firsts. Nothing like it. But then we began the second year, where we are today, and it's a different kind of sucks. People have gone back to living their lives. Yes, they check in...many do. But honestly, everyone resumes life just as it was before. It's the ones that have to live with the loss, day in and day out, who cannot just go back to living life as it was before. Yes, we move forward. We work. We travel. We play. We get used to a new way of carrying on, but we don't want to get used to it. At the end of the day, there is this loss. This silence in my heart.

Every day when I come home, I am aware that I only have one child present...not two. Every night I climb into my bed, the place where Tanner took his last breath, and I take a deep breath. Every night, I wake up in the middle of the night. I don't remember the last time I slept a full night. Sometimes I wake up calling his name, half expecting him to answer. Life is so different. Life will never be the same.

Last week, on Mother's Day, a friend of mine posted a picture with his son. I looked at that picture for the longest time, both with tears and smiles. I could feel the love between this parent and child. I could feel the warmth between them. How close they were, touching each other, their smiles radiating that love. I so wanted to trade places with them. For Tanner to become the son. For me to become my friend. Trade places and remember that warmth. What I would give to have that again.

I have learned so much…more than I ever expected. I feel that I have gotten smarter, quicker on my feet. I say what I want to say (and yes, that can get me in trouble)…but, in many ways, I don't care. Life is short and we shouldn't waste a single minute. Be with the one you love. Take risks. Take chances. Smell the flowers (even the calla lilies). Breathe in the ocean air. Be happy. Smile. Eat dessert. Laugh as you've never laughed before. Don't take no for an answer. Make your dreams come true. Light the fire, even if it's eighty degrees. Go outside the box. Be yourself. Believe in yourself. Be amazing. Create amazing. Do it all.

Tanner's illness and death helped me conquer so much. In all honesty, I didn't think I was strong enough to be the person who could go through everything that I did; to be the person

I am today. At that moment in the emergency room, when the doctor shut the door and told us to sit down, my life changed. When Tanner took his last breath, my life changed. I have become much more powerful than I ever imagined...powerful and with the strength to get me through the impossible.

5.21.15

Two years today ago we saw the rainbow around the sun.

A friend texted me a quote the other day which read: "I didn't expect to lose so much of myself, when I lost you. I'll spend the rest of my life learning who I've become and wondering who you would have been." How true.

You have kids...you build a family. You protect them and love them, you nurture and discipline them, you teach and show and encourage them, you help them and comfort them. You are their parent...their mom...their dad. They need you...and you need them. They are your life...an extension of you...a part of your heart and soul. You pray that your children grow up to be happy and healthy...healthy and happy. You never expect the worst to happen. And then it does...

When Tanner died, I lost a part of me. A permanent part that will never grow back. When your kids go off to summer camp, they come back. When your kids go to college, they come back.

Rainbow Around The Son

When they move away, they still come back and visit. If you're divorced and only get to see your kids half the time, you still continue to see them. The point is this…yes, it's hard to adjust to change. To accept something new and know your kids will not always be around 24/7…but they are still here. You can still see them. You can still visit them. You can still hold them. Comfort them. Kiss them. Hug them. They come back….your kids come back. People like me…parents who have lost a child…would give anything for the "coming back."

Instead, every day I think about how to put one foot in front of the other. I think about what each day will bring. I think about how strong I am, even though deep inside I'm curled in a ball. A part of me is gone…forever. I will never be the person I was. Never. That's a tough one. Something I struggle with every day.

People tell me their stories. Close friends tell me stories that Tanner is a part of. My friend's son rocking out to "My Hero." Friends who dream of talking to Tanner. Stories of rainbows, taxicabs and elevators. All of those stories mean the world to me, and I don't think they are accidental. I truly believe Tanner is there…meeting my friends in their dreams, rocking out with my friend's kid. Tanner is there with them, because he knows these people will tell me. He chooses the people I love, knowing they will tell me their stories, and that, they will make his Mama smile.

I have many pictures of Tanner throughout my home, but there is one in my office that I particularly love. I feel him through this picture. It's from a photo booth, taken the summer before he got sick. His eyes smile at me. I analyze his face, his goofy smile, his expression, but I also search for any sign of what was to come. Should have I seen something? I knew him so well...should I have known? There is nothing. Nothing in that picture which hints at our future.

My emotions, my thoughts, my sadness comes in waves. I run on the beach, listen to my music and something...anything...the surf, a bird, a rock, a seashell...can trigger the tears. I drive down the 405 freeway, and as I pass the cemetery, I always wave and blow a kiss, and my heart skips a beat. I might be in my office... deep in work...and I look up...see his picture, and my life just stops for a moment. How can it be? I ask myself that so many times a day. How can it be?

I seem strong. And honestly, I am very strong. But even the strongest...even the bravest...crash. I always take one step in front of the other. I don't stop. But there are times, that I take that step and my heart falls. The tears fall. I break. And it's okay...I let it happen. It's just that it happens more than anyone knows or realizes.

Rainbow Around The Son

The emptiness in my heart is always there. The loss of a child is something one never gets past. Time doesn't make it easier. Time doesn't make it better; in fact, it becomes worse. But we have no choice. Life goes on. Life doesn't stop for anything. The sadness, the emptiness, missing Tanner, is constant. We may smile. We may laugh. We may dance. We may sing. We may drink. We may have fun. We may run off to Vegas for the night. We may play. We may love. But the loss remains. Always and forever...we will never be complete again.

5.22.15

I have made it past and am on the other side of the week of heartbreak. Yesterday marked two years since the funeral. I went to the cemetery and stood over Tanner's grave, the same spot where I stood two years ago. I looked up at the sky and it was different than it had been that day. There were clouds and it was breezy. The sun was out, but it was not too hot. I looked up to see if I could find a glimpse of a rainbow. Of course, it was not there.

I juggle a lot. Mourning Tanner and keeping Casey healthy. I have lost one child, and I will not lose another. Every day I focus on making sure Casey is safe and healthy, doing my best to make sure she lives a normal teenage life. I also know that when she's off to college in the next few years, I'm going to have to let her go...at least to a point. I can't be there to make sure she is healthy on a daily basis. That will be up to her. She will have to be aware of her body, of what feels normal and what doesn't. All I can do, as a parent, like so many parents out there, is prepare her and hope everything will be okay.

I lead by example. So Casey will know how to do the right thing. She already emulates me in so many ways. It's important that she models herself on someone who knows it's okay to laugh and smile and also feel sad and cry. I show her that I am strong, but also that it's okay to break down. I show her the importance of speaking up, speaking out and saying what's on your mind. I show her how to be a strong and independent woman. And I show her it's okay to fall as long as we always get up.

Life does go on...as much as it hurts...it does go on. I show her that, too. I have always felt that the healthiest way to deal with our tragedy is to talk about it. To share and express our feelings. I think, at the end of the day, I've done a pretty damn good job.

I have no regrets. I've said it before, and I'll say it again...no regrets. I did everything I could for Tanner. Everything...and so much more. Maybe that's what helps me get through my pain, through each day...having no regrets.

I do want to feel again. That is what I want. To feel good again. To close my eyes, get lost, to imagine and hope and love and remember. To feel peace. To feel serenity. To feel okay. I want to sparkle again. And I will. I know I will.

There is no handbook. There are no rules. The truth is nothing can change what's happened. We can't go back. Only forward. So it's all about figuring out *how* to go forward.

At the end of the day, no one saved me. I saved myself. Through the strength of Tanner, through the strength I didn't even know I had...I saved myself. And as sad as I am, as lost as I sometimes feel and as often as I don't recognize myself...I think I'm doing okay. Not great. Not bad. Okay. And every day is a step closer to being a little better than okay.

I pulled into the driveway this morning, and there it was again...the calla lily. I think this time I will leave it alone. I will not be afraid. I will allow it to grow and blossom in all its beauty.

Maybe it's time I start doing the same for myself. xo

Epilogue

It has been over five years since Tanner died. Over six years since he was diagnosed.

Casey is almost twenty years old and a very happy and thriving college sophomore. When Casey was a junior in high school, she went public about her mutant p53 gene and has since launched her initiative, Genome Generation (www.genomegeneration.com), to raise awareness about the importance of knowing your family's health history. She was also featured on "NBC Nightly News with Lester Holt," and Amy Poehler's Smart Girls. She continues to be sweet, amazing and beautiful. Thankfully, she remains healthy.

Greg also remains healthy. I am fortunate to have an ex-husband, who is a great friend and co-parent. Even with Casey away at college, we still talk and text and sometimes get together for dinner…yes, just the two of us.

The Tanner Project Foundation (www.tannerproject.org) concluded the N-of-1 project at JCVI, and I have been given the tools and information to continue implementing their protocol to keep Casey healthy. We support doctors, who work in cancer research using innovative measures and who continue to think outside the box, including Dr. Joshua Schiffman of Huntsman Cancer Institute and Dr. Santosh Kesari of John Wayne Cancer Institute, where I am proud to sit on his Brain Trust Committee.

The Tanner Project Foundation is currently conducting a medical technology project, which mines the Dark Data of brain and whole-body imaging, using emerging AI deep learning technologies to hopefully predict data patterns, years before disease begins. We call this technology, *Stage 0.*

I do believe that my voice needs to be heard on the importance of knowing one's family genetics (knowledge is power!) and being proactive. In 2017, I was honored to be included on a panel at the Milken Institute Global Conference. Afterwards, someone approached me and said, "What the other panelists had to say was interesting, but Marlo, what you said…people will take home with them." If anything sums it up, it is that. My message is powerful and resonates with so many.

I have had other speaking engagements, including being one of the keynote speakers in Washington, D.C. for the Coalition for Imaging and Bioengineering Research (CIBR). My hope is that my words will inspire, educate and encourage others. I know there's so much more in store for me. I have only just begun to make a difference.

During the past few years, I have learned not only to appreciate every day, but to look at the "amazing" of every day. Even through my sadness and loss, I am looking for the "amazing." It doesn't have to be revolutionary or life changing, just something that makes you smile or laugh, appreciate or enjoy. So, I have been doing a little feel-good project: "Create Amazing," and post daily on Instagram (@howdoyoucreateamazing). It can be the sunrise or sunset, ocean waves, fresh flowers, a fabulous dessert, a glass of wine, your favorite quote or song lyric, a great meal...simple daily actions which catch your eye and make you Create Amazing. Try it and ask yourself: How do you Create Amazing?

I still write on Facebook, although not as much as I used to. I know people miss my posts. They tell me so. They have told me my words have inspired them. That my words have given them pause. That my words have made them think, grow, learn and love. I appreciate that, and maybe that's one of the reasons I decided to write this book...so I can share all of my thoughts and feelings in one place.

I miss Tanner with all of my heart. The hurt, the sadness, the disbelief is, of course, all still there. And the waves still hit when you least expect them. I was at a dance recital recently, and in the darkness of the auditorium, I saw a little boy crawl into his mom's lap. I watched him snuggle his head against her chest. I watched her place her cheek against his hair. I kept my composure, but the tears flowed. I miss that. I miss that feeling...so much. Yes, it is still so very sad. I don't think there will ever be a time when it is not. Those waves are always going to hit. But what can I do? It is what it is...and life goes on.

I talk about Tanner all the time. I want his memory to be ever-present. I know my generation, my friends will always remember him...of course, they will. My greatest hope is that his generation, his friends, his classmates, my friends' kids, also always remember Tanner. And that one day they will grow up and tell their children about their friend, Tanner, who made them laugh and smile.

I am officially an empty nester...sooner than I should be. Yes, there are some sad moments, but, all in all, it's not as bad as I thought. My home is quiet...sometimes it's too quiet, but usually it's a good quiet. And, if I'm being honest here, "good quiet" is good...really good.

For the first time in a long time, I can do what I want...when I want. There's something to be said about having that freedom. I can watch my shows. Make dinner or order in. Go in the hot tub at midnight. Dance around my living room naked. Sing my heart out. Blast Dave Matthews Band. I write. I work out. I go to the cemetery about once a week and always bring fresh flowers. I have helped others who have suffered loss...showing them they are not alone...which in turn has really helped me. I see my family. I keep my heart open.

I create new memories. I go out with my friends. I'm fortunate to have my oldest friends still by my side, but I have also made new, great friendships that I know will last a lifetime. I spend time with Michael enjoying long walks, long drives, great meals, laughter and fun. I love being with Casey and watching her grow into the young woman she is becoming. I say Tanner's name out loud, just so I can hear the sound of it. I still like red wine, but am learning to love tequila. And...I smile more.

Am I happy? Honestly, I don't know if I will ever have complete happiness again. But yeah...I think I'm getting there. xo

www.ingramcontent.com/pod-product-compliance
Lightning Source LLC
Chambersburg PA
CBHW052014070526
44584CB00016B/1747